PROTECTING
YOUR SONGS & YOURSELF

PROTECTING
YOUR SONGS & YOURSELF

Kent J. Klavens

Cincinnati, Ohio

Protecting Your Songs and Yourself. Copyright © 1989 by Kent J. Klavens. Printed and bound in the United States of America. All rights reserved. No part of this book may be reproduced in any form or by any electronic or mechanical means including information storage and retrieval systems without permission in writing from the publisher, except by a reviewer, who may quote brief passages in a review. Published by Writer's Digest Books, an imprint of F&W Publications, Inc., 1507 Dana Avenue, Cincinnati, Ohio 45207. First edition.

93 92 91 90 89   5 4 3 2 1

Library of Congress Cataloging in Publication Data

Klavens, Kent J., 1949—
    Protecting your songs and yourself: the songwriter's legal guide /by Kent J. Klavens.
        p.   cm.
    Includes index.
    ISBN 0-89879-364-5
    1. Copyright—Music—United States—Popular works. 2. Composers—Legal status, laws, etc.—United States—Popular works.   I. Title.
KF3035.Z9K55   1989
346.7304'82—dc20   89-16451
[347.306482]   CIP

ACKNOWLEDGMENTS

Before I dive into the legal issues of songwriting, I'd like to thank my editor, Julie Wesling Whaley—not only for her expert editorial advice, but for encouraging me to start writing this book and giving me enough continuing encouragement to finish it.

Thanks also go to my office assistant, Jackie Duhovic, and independent editor, Chris Dodd, for their many hours of proofreading and editing, as well as attorney Shirley Bennett, who gave me some valuable, last minute opinions on my tax law chapter.

The most special thanks go to all of the songwriters I've represented over the years. Their creative energy, tireless dreams, and endless devotion to the craft of songwriting were the ultimate inspiration for this book.

This book is dedicated to my parents, without whose love, guidance, and support over the years, my life and this book would not have been possible, and to Cheryl, whose love has made the future appear brighter than ever before.

CONTENTS

BEFORE WE BEGIN

When I was first asked to write this book, my initial reaction was total panic! I had written many articles for magazines on legal topics in the music industry, but they had always been short, to-the-point, and easy to digest. Now I would be given the opportunity, in one place, to endlessly discuss a variety of important legal topics concerning songwriters. How could I possibly create something that would be not only useful, but interesting and easy to read? My image of law books had always been that they were boring and confusing for law students and attorneys and totally incomprehensible to anyone else!

This book should provide a basic legal background for songwriters and anyone wanting to represent songwriters, but it's not intended as a complete guide for law students or attorneys. It's primarily for those of you who *are* songwriters, and I've tried to give you enough information to understand and recognize the major legal and business issues that affect your songs. Having represented hundreds of songwriters in my law practice, I've seen many of them waste money on legal fees for either simple problems or problems they should have been able to avoid.

If you use this book, will you be able to get along without ever using an attorney? Of course not. Even though much of the advice will save you unnecessary legal fees by keeping you away from certain problems, other information is specifically intended to help you recognize when you need professional legal help. Think of this book like you would a home medical guide. You'll learn when you just have a cold and can purchase aspirin for yourself, and you'll also become aware of the symptoms of diseases that require a doctor's care. Perhaps most important, you'll learn how to stay well!

Also like a home medical guide, I'm not going to teach you how to perform surgery on yourself. After reading this book you'll be able to negotiate some of the major deal points for most kinds of agreements involving your songs, but you'll still need an attorney to draft and review the written agreements. That's why I haven't included any of the form contracts you usually see in this type of book.

In my experience, many people are quick to rely on form agreements to save money. Those kinds of documents are virtually always drafted too generally, and they are either used incorrectly or are inadequate for the purpose intended. I've known songwriters who have taken form music publishing agreements from books and given them to music publishers, even though the forms were clearly drafted in favor of the publisher! A classic example of a usually inadequate form agreement would be a form collaboration agreement for two songwriters creating a song together. As you'll see when you read the chapter on collaboration, there are many different factors to be considered in these agreements, and I've never seen a form collaboration agreement that covers all the legal issues and possible concerns for the songwriters involved.

When you *do* need an attorney, where do you go? First, I'll tell you where *not* to go. Regardless of how much money you'll save, don't rely on the legal advice and contract drafting skill of attorneys in your family like your Uncle Fred, the tax lawyer; your Aunt Anita, the divorce lawyer; your sister Mary, the corporate lawyer; your brother Bob, the criminal lawyer; your cousin Elmer, the real estate lawyer; or any other relative, friend, or attorney, *unless they are experienced in music industry matters*. Although they might be able to read a contract about your songs and tell you what it says and what it means, they won't be able to tell you what it *should* say and what normal protective language might be missing. They also won't know the normal percentages and royalties for the music industry and how they are defined and computed. So if you rely on relatives or friends for specialized legal advice in the music industry, and if they don't really know the field, you will probably cost yourself a lot of money and heartache in the future.

The vast majority of experienced, full-time music industry attorneys are located in Los Angeles, New York City, and Nashville. It's always possible to do business by phone and mail with these people, and you can always get referrals from songwriter organizations such as the National Academy of Songwriters and the Los Angeles Songwriters Showcase (located in Los Angeles), The Songwriters Guild of America (with offices in New York, Nashville, and Los Angeles), the Nashville Songwriters Association, International (located in Nashville), and ASCAP and BMI (these are performing rights organizations with offices in the three major music cities and other locations). The addresses and telephone numbers of these organizations are listed in chapter four. You should also be able to find attorneys who work at least part-time in the music industry in other cities that have a visible level of national music industry activity. These might include Chicago, San Francisco, Boston, Detroit, Philadelphia, Atlanta, and Memphis.

I've started this book with a chapter discussing copyright laws because they provide the basis for all rights, agreements, and other legal issues that affect your songs—it's a fundamental background for the rest of the book. Therefore, although it's probably the most difficult chapter to read, it's important to try to understand as much as possible before going on. Throughout the book, don't let any legal terminology or other unfamiliar words I've used intimidate you. If you're going to be a professional songwriter, you need to know the language of the business. All of these terms are explained in either the chapter where they first appear or in a later chapter. The same is true for particular legal or business concepts. A concept that may be too difficult for you to tackle in one chapter may become clearer after you've read a later chapter, so keep reading!

Why should this book be important to you? To maximize your success as a creative artist, you must be aware of the business and legal reality that affects what you do. I've known far too many songwriters who have lost valuable opportunities (or pursued the wrong opportunities) because they didn't know the fundamental laws and business principles affecting the craft of songwriting. There are even successful songwriters and major superstars who regret some foolish deals they made many years ago, because they realize now that they substantially reduced their income from some of their best early songs.

When you finish this book, you'll know more about the legal and business aspects of songwriting than the majority of songwriters. Most important, you'll know how to avoid legal disasters. That alone should make the reading well worth the effort.

CHAPTER 1

COPYRIGHT LAW:
THE PRIMARY SOURCE OF YOUR RIGHTS

No matter what your level of songwriting experience or success, you should make an effort to tackle at least the basic concepts of the copyright laws. Virtually all of the legal rights you own in your songs come from these laws, and whenever you sign any kind of agreement affecting your songs, you will be dealing with some or all of these rights. This will be the most technical area of the book, so don't be worried. The rest is easy!

When Is a Song Protected?

The Copyright Law of the United States provides a variety of legal rights and protection to the creator of an *original work of authorship*. For your songs, then, it is important to understand the meaning of *originality* and what constitutes a *work of authorship*.

Originality for a song simply requires that you create original music and lyrics. If you create original lyrics alone or original music alone, these can be separately protected under the copyright law. To be original, your music and lyrics must not have been substantially copied from any other song that is protected by copyright and must also contain some degree of novelty or distinctiveness. As to what is *substantial* copying, juries and judges determine that on a case-by-case basis. There are no maximum or minimum numbers of notes, words, or musical bars that may or may not be copied. If you think that you may be copying someone else's work, don't do it! (There will be a more thorough discussion of copyright *infringement* later in this chapter.)

As long as you have not substantially copied lyrics or music from a protected song, it is not really difficult to meet the originality criteria for copyright. Be aware, however, that if you create a distinctive melody line with lyrics that include nothing more than a repetition of the same two words throughout the song (for example, "Let's dance! Let's dance!"), those lyrics will not be protected by the copyright law unless someone uses them with the same melodic notes and rhythm contained in your song.

For your creation to be considered a *work of authorship*, there must be an expression of your original musical or lyrical creation that has been *fixed* in *tangible* form. This simply means that a mere idea for a song (such as one about two next-door neighbors who fall in love) will not be protected until actually expressed with specific lyrics and music that have been embodied in some medium of recorded expression (for example, written down on paper or recorded on tape). Even when expressed in tangible form, however, titles, phrases, and other short expressions are not protected

> To be original, your music and lyrics must not have been substantially copied from any other song that is protected by copyright and must also contain some degree of novelty or distinctiveness.

by copyright, so don't attempt to register and protect two lines of lyrics or a few bars of music as a separate work of authorship.

Remember that your song is protected under the copyright laws immediately upon its *fixation* in tangible form. Formal *registration* in Washington, D.C. only provides evidence of your claim and makes available to you certain other legal procedural advantages if you sue someone for copying (infringing) your work. I'll discuss more specifics on registering your copyright later in this chapter.

The *term* (duration) of copyright protection is for the life of the author plus fifty years (in the case of songs created by two or more songwriters, this is marked from the death of the last surviving writer). For *works made for hire* (I'll describe this later), the duration of copyright is seventy-five years from *publication* (a legal term specifically defined in the law that I'll also discuss later) or one hundred years from creation, whichever is shorter.

What Parts of a Song Are Protected?

For purposes of copyright protection, the primary source of originality usually involves only the melody line and lyrics. Rhythm has rarely been found to be original enough in itself to be protected by copyright, although the rhythm is certainly taken into consideration in determining the degree of similarity between two melody lines. Harmony is also virtually never protected.

A musical arrangement *may* be protected by copyright, but a very high degree of originality is required. Also, an arrangement of a song is a *derivative right* (a right derived from the original song), so the copyright owner of the song must consent to ownership of a separate copyright for the arrangement. Most copyright owners will not permit this. Assuming sufficient originality, an arrangement of a song in the *public domain* (that is, a song not protected by copyright) is the most likely type of arrangement to merit separate copyright protection for the arranger.

The other most common copyright in the music industry, a sound recording copyright, is a different matter because it protects the actual sounds on a recording against unauthorized reproduction. These copyrights are most often held by record companies, who have usually obtained all rights to the performances of the musical and vocal performers on the sound recording as well as to the services of the record producer who processed and compiled all of the performances and other sounds and put them in the final recording.

What Songs Are Not Protected?

Besides mere ideas for music or lyrics, or certain forms of expression that do not constitute original works of authorship, there are many existing songs that may not be protected by copyright. These are considered to be *in the public domain*, and anyone may use as much as they like from such songs in creating a new song (of course, the "free" elements taken from the prior song will not be protected in the new song either). For example, compositions written by Mozart are not protected by the copyright laws, so you could use a pretty melody from one of his works for your love ballad without needing anyone's permission. If someone else later wanted to copy the same melody line from your song, however, they would not need your permission either, although they could not take any of the original, protectible lyrics or music you created for the song.

Whether or not a song is in the public domain can be a difficult question. This is because the U.S. Copyright Law was revised substantially in the late 1970s (effective on January 1, 1978), drastically changing the term of copyright protection and the registration requirements, and was further revised when the United States joined the Berne Convention (an international copyright treaty) in 1989. Prior to these revisions to the law, for example, a song was not protected under federal copyright law at all until it was properly registered in the Copyright Office (although certain state laws may have protected these songs); a song could have been in the public domain if it was *published* prior to proper registration without an appropriate copyright notice. Now a song is protected from the moment it is fixed in tangible form, regardless of registration, and a song published without proper copyright notice cannot "fall" into the public domain. Also, there used to be an *initial* copyright term of twenty-eight years and a separate *renewal* term of an additional twenty-eight years as opposed to the present term described earlier.

To confuse matters more, under the revised copyright laws, there is one set of rules and requirements for the copyright term of songs that were in their initial copyright term on January 1, 1978, another set of rules for songs in their renewal term on that date, and a third set of rules for works created thereafter. So a determination of whether a song is in the public domain could depend upon when it was created, when it was registered for copyright, when it was published, and whether its copyright was properly renewed.

If you need to know whether an old song is still protected by copyright, contact either an attorney or the Copyright Office regarding investigation of the copyright status of that song.

Who Owns a Song's Copyright?

The creator of a song owns the copyright unless that copyright has been transferred either by *operation of law* (without a written agreement) or by the terms of a written document. It's important to know that it's not always necessary for you to have signed a contract for there to have been a partial or complete transfer of ownership rights to your song. These types of *automatic* transfers of rights include the following:

> The creator of a song owns the copyright unless that copyright has been transferred either by *operation of law* (without a written agreement) or by the terms of a written document.

1. The most common *partial* transfer of rights by operation of law occurs when a song is created jointly by more than one songwriter. Without a written document specifying otherwise, all of the songwriters are equal, joint owners. (I'll be discussing this and other collaboration issues in chapter three.)
2. Another way in which a song copyright is transferred by operation of law is when a song was created as a *work made for hire*. Unless a song was created by the songwriter as an employee within the "scope" of employment, this type of transfer will not occur without a written agreement specifying that a songwriter is creating (or has created) a *work made for hire*. Typically, to avoid any dispute as to whether a particular creative relationship was really one of employment, a written agreement usually *will* be requested in this situation.

In all *work made for hire* relationships, the employer (whether a person or company) acquiring the song is considered the author for all purposes.

If a situation like this is proposed to you, you must be careful to retain both the right to future royalties from exploitation of the song, which I'll discuss in chapter six, and a guarantee of printed or visual credit for writing the song. An appropriate contractual provision might specify that the credit appear "wherever such credit normally appears for songwriters in the entertainment industry."

Aside from *exclusive* or *staff* songwriter agreements (discussed in chapter seven), or agreements with film, television, home video, or commercial advertising production companies to compose scores or songs for a specific project in exchange for an advance fee, you should virtually never agree that a song you've created will be considered written for hire. For example, a song you create *before* you present it for consideration in a film, television, home video, or commercial project should *not* be characterized as work made for hire. Even though you might agree to assign (transfer ownership) the copyright for the song to the production company anyway, you will retain greater rights if the song is not deemed created for hire. You should have work made for hire language deleted from any songwriting agreement where it appears to be inappropriate.

3. A third way in which a song copyright may apparently be partially transferred by operation of law is under the community property laws that exist in various states. In states with such laws, property created or acquired by either a husband or wife during marriage automatically becomes the joint property of the spouses.

    A 1987 California state court case appears to have been the first to conclusively determine that such laws apply to copyrights, and that the copyright in a song is jointly owned by the spouses immediately upon creation of the song in fixed form by either the husband or the wife. Many legal theorists have criticized that case for the unresolved problems it creates, so by the time you read this book, either a federal court or other court in your state may have reached a different legal conclusion. Nonetheless, married songwriters should be aware of the possible legal issues.

Some of the potential problems raised by the apparent effect of community property laws on copyrights include the following:
- If both spouses are equal co-owners of the copyright created by one of them, it's logical that the copyright *notice* (a written legend on visible copies of the song) should include both names or the name of a company owned by both. Is a copyright notice reflecting only the songwriter spouse an improper notice?
- Community property laws often have specific provisions affecting the management of community property that appear to contradict the provisions of the copyright laws. For example, in California, a spouse with primary management and control of the community property can make certain transfers of community property without the consent of the other spouse. Under the copyright laws, no co-owner of a copyright can transfer another co-owner's ownership interest without written consent. Can a songwriting spouse legally sign a music publishing agreement for the entire ownership interest in a song without the non-songwriting spouse's signature?

There are other legal issues affecting the management and control of copyrights between spouses living in community property states that are far too complex for further discussion here. If you think these laws might affect you, the safest solution would be for you to request that your non-songwriting spouse sign a *power of attorney* giving you the total right, power, and authority to enter into any form of agreement whatsoever (including complete transfers of copyrights) affecting songs created during the marriage without the approval of your non-songwriting spouse. (See an attorney for the appropriate language.)

If you intend to present your spouse with the type of document described above, you may want to preserve marital harmony (no pun intended) by making it clear that you are not trying to take away your spouse's rights to income from any songs — you only want the legally clear, exclusive power to determine when and how your songs will be used and transferred.

Other than by operation of law, a transfer of the copyright in a song must be made in a written document. Oral agreements to transfer ownership are void and unenforceable.

Other than by operation of law, a transfer of the copyright in a song must be made in a written document. Oral agreements to transfer ownership are void and unenforceable.

What Rights Are Involved In Copyright?

The rights involved in copyright are simply your exclusive rights to do anything you want with your song (assuming you don't violate some other law in the process, such as performing a song with obscene lyrics over public airwaves). You should always remember that, with certain limited exceptions (such as *fair use* for purposes of education, criticism, or commentary), *no one can exercise any of these rights without your permission*. The most common rights include:

1. *Mechanical Rights* — These are the rights to mechanically reproduce the song on records, tapes, compact discs, and other recorded products. It is important to know about *compulsory mechanical licenses*, because it's the major area in music copyrights where someone does *not* need your permission to use your song. Once a song has been distributed for sale to the public in the U.S. in the form of *phonorecords* (a term specifically defined in the Copyright Law that includes virtually all recorded products now commonly exploited except audio-visual products), *anyone* can produce and record that song (not the original recorded performance, though) for other phonorecords *without approval*, as long as they comply with the law regarding proper notice, payment, and accounting to the music publisher or songwriter controlling the rights.

   The royalty that is paid is known as the *statutory royalty* (which, as this book is written, is 5¼ cents per song per phonorecord copy sold. Under current law that rate will adjust periodically under a formula tied to the Consumer Price Index.) So if you want to "cover" a particular song of a major artist that you really love, you can do it without permission if you follow the legal requirements and pay the statutory royalty.

2. *Synchronization Rights* — These are the rights to synchronize the song with visual action for a television program, theatrical motion picture, home video device, or other filmed, taped, or reproduced visual action.

3. *Print Rights* — These are the rights to print sheet music and other visual copies of the song.

4. *Small Performing Rights* — These are certain, specifically defined performances of your music that are distinguished from other performing rights primarily because two major performing rights "societies" (ASCAP and BMI) collect the vast majority of these sums for their songwriter and publisher members. *Small performances* mostly include performances on radio and television, and in motion picture theaters outside the U.S., nightclubs, concert halls, and commercial businesses (for example, recorded music performed in jukeboxes, elevators, and department stores). As a practical matter, you will not be paid for these rights unless you have become a member of some performing rights society, because it would be too difficult for you to go around the country suing everyone who is performing your hit song without your permission. By joining either ASCAP or BMI (you can't belong to both as a songwriter), or by using some other collection organization (for example, SESAC), you have a *collection agent* granting permission for these performances and collecting money on your behalf.

5. *Grand Performing Rights* — This term is most often applied to the *dramatic performance* of music in musical plays. It is also sometimes described to include the dramatic performance of a song in any manner that advances the plot or story line of the "work" in which it is performed. As a practical matter, though, the dramatic performance of songs in a theatrical motion picture or television program (for example, a motion picture or television performance of a musical such as *Fiddler on the Roof*) usually generates separate small performing rights payments. The grand performing right for such programs is most often covered in the fee paid for the synchronization right for the song.

6. *Derivative Rights* — These are the rights to create other works *derived* from the song, such as television commercials and new foreign lyrical versions. In the case of the "Ode to Billie Joe," an entire motion picture was based upon a song. All of these derivative "works" require the permission of the copyright owner of the original song.

7. *General Exploitation and Administration Rights* — These are the rights to issue the licenses (permissions) for all of the uses described above, as well as to collect the money from the exercise of all of the rights to the song. These rights are commonly transferred if you are assigning your song's copyright to a music publisher. It is also common to assign these rights to a foreign subpublisher for a particular country or region of the world.

Derivative Rights are the rights to create other works *derived* from the song, such as television commercials and new foreign lyrical versions.

The administration and negotiation of the major rights areas I've just described will be discussed in greater detail in chapter nine on self-publishing.

What Is Copyright Infringement?

For songs, an *infringement* is generally any unauthorized use of a substantial part of a song that is not within some exception in the Copyright Law allowing that use (such as *fair use* for educational purposes). For this section, though, I will concentrate only on infringement in the creation of a song, because situations such as the sale of "bootleg" copies by record counterfeiters or some other unlawful use of an entire song without authorization are too obvious to merit discussion. In the next chapter,

I'll cover other limitations to creating songs and demos, including parodies of existing songs, and the use of *sampling* in the creation of demos; I'll also discuss how a song's lyrics might be considered defamatory or violate someone's *right of publicity*.

In the most basic sense, copyright infringement with respect to creation of a song is the copying of one legally protected song in the creation of another song. A legal finding of this kind of infringement generally requires proof of both *access* to the copyrighted song and *substantial similarity* between the protected song and the later song.

Proof of *access*, or at least proof that an infringing songwriter had the reasonable opportunity to hear and copy the protected song, can be critical. Some courts have permitted two songs to have striking similarity (that is, the two songs were even *more* than substantially similar) without a legal finding of copyright infringement because the copyright laws theoretically permit two different songwriters, creating songs independently of each other, to create virtually identical songs, both capable of copyright protection.

A songwriter named Selle once sued the Bee Gees for copyright infringement, claiming "How Deep Is Your Love" infringed his song "Let It End." A musical expert testified that twenty-four of the first thirty-four notes of the Bee Gees' song were identical to Selle's song. In fact, the similarity between the songs was so blatant that one of the Bee Gees, while on the witness stand, mistakenly identified music from "Let It End" as music from "How Deep Is Your Love"! The judge in that case reversed a jury finding of copyright infringement primarily because Selle could offer only speculation and conjecture as to how the Bee Gees had the opportunity to hear and copy his song.

> Keep an accurate, precise record of every person and company where you have sent a demo tape of your songs, as well as the names of the songs on each tape.

The importance of this principle to the songwriter is obvious: Keep an accurate, precise record of every person and company where you have sent a demo tape of your songs, as well as the names of the songs on each tape. All of this evidence could prove crucial if you ever sue someone for copyright infringement.

Of course, if a hit song is widely known and performed, no particular evidence that an infringing songwriter heard or copied the song will be necessary. George Harrison was held liable for copyright infringement in creating "My Sweet Lord" based on its substantial similarity to the hit song "He's So Fine." The widespread popularity of "He's So Fine" led to a finding that, even if George Harrison did not intentionally copy it, he must have heard the song at some point and copied it subconsciously.

What is *substantial similarity* between two songs? Contrary to the belief of many songwriters that they can safely use up to two or three bars or eight notes of another song (or some other absolute number), this is not the case. There is no definite test. For most courts in this country, even though the testimony of musical experts will virtually always be introduced as evidence during a trial involving copyright infringement, the test will be a *question of fact* for a judge or a jury to decide after hearing both songs.

What Is Publication of a Song?

The legal concept of *publication* is important in the copyright law, because the actual date of publication will affect the copyright registration procedure for the song, the "presumption" of legal validity for the facts stated in the copyright registration, the necessity of copyright notice, the proper form of notice, the term of copyright protection, the availability of certain legal "remedies" in case of infringement, and various other legal rights you will have to your song. The most important of these are discussed throughout this chapter. The actual legal definition is the following:

Publication is the distribution of copies or phonorecords of a work to the public by sale or other transfer of ownership, or by rental, lease, or lending. The offering to distribute copies of phonorecords to a group of persons for purposes of further distribution, public performance, or public display constitutes publication. A public performance or display of a work does not of itself constitute publication.

The first commonly misunderstood aspect of this concept is that merely signing your song to a music publisher is *not* publication and does *not* mean your song has been published within the meaning of the copyright law. Also, a single performance of your song, whether on radio or television, or the multiple performances of the song live at local nightclubs, does not, *by itself*, constitute publication. If you distribute multiple copies for purposes of public performance, though, that *would* be considered publication (for example, sending copies of records to many radio stations or copies of videos to many television stations).

Although there have been no major cases on the subject under the current version of the copyright laws, it appears that limited distribution of demo tapes to music publishers or record companies for promotional purposes is not considered legal publication. Even though the *eventual* purpose of that kind of promotion is the distribution and public performance of the songs on the tapes to the public, that kind of distribution is limited both as to specific people to whom they are being sent and to the immediate purpose of promotion. If the distribution were for the *direct* purpose of further distribution (for example, distribution of actual sale copies to a record distributor for further distribution to retailers for further sale to the public) or for the *direct* purpose of public performance (for example, distribution of a motion picture containing the song to movie theaters for exhibition to the public), then publication will have legally occurred.

Bear in mind that, despite the discussion in the paragraph above, if a songwriter were to send hundreds of copies of a song over a long period of time to various publishers, managers, record companies, producers, and recording artists, a court would likely find that a legal publication had occurred. There is no precise dividing line as to how many copies would have to be sent for this to occur. If you are in doubt, consider the song to have been published and follow all of the copyright registration and copyright notice procedures described in this chapter and in the informational materials available from the Copyright Office.

How Are Copyrights Registered?

Registration of copyright in a song is accomplished by filing the proper form with the Register of Copyrights in Washington, D.C., paying the filing fee (currently ten dollars), and submitting either one or two copies of the work to be registered. Generally, one copy is required if the song is unpublished, and two are required if the song has

Merely signing your song to a music publisher is *not* publication and does *not* mean your song has been published within the meaning of the copyright law.

been published. Copyright forms may be obtained by writing to the Copyright Office, Library of Congress, Washington, D.C. 20559. As this chapter is being written, there is also a direct telephone number for ordering forms: (202) 287-9100. 707 - 9100

Form PA is usually the proper form to use for a song. A form SR should be used to obtain a *sound recording copyright* if you wish to protect the actual sounds on your tape or record in addition to the music and lyrics registered. For example, you may have used some unique synthesizer sounds on your track that you programmed after weeks of work. Although individual sounds are not protected under a song copyright, a sound recording copyright, or under the copyright laws in general, the collection and compilation of various sounds in an original manner would be protected. Anyone could *imitate* those sounds without consequences, but if they copy (dub) a substantial part of the actual sounds from your tape, you would have a right of legal action against them.

The copyright office does not require either a lead sheet or lyric sheet along with your tape. It is usually best to submit these as extra protection, however, because your registration is only effective for exactly what you register. If any of the lyrics or melody line to your song are not clear on the tape you submit with your registration form, and if you are later involved in a legal action concerning those unclear elements in particular, it's possible you will have totally lost the advantages of copyright registration relating to those elements.

To save money, multiple songs can be registered on one tape as a *collection* for one fee of ten dollars, and you can use a title such as *The Best of (your name), Part I* or *Songs of Love*. The Copyright Office requires that, to register two or more unpublished musical compositions with one application and fee, *all* of the following conditions must be met:

1. the songs must be assembled in an orderly form;
2. the combined songs must bear a single title identifying the collection as a whole;
3. the copyright "claimant" or claimants must be the same for each song (that is, the owner or owners of the copyright for each song must be the same); and
4. all of the songs must be by the same songwriter, or, if they are by different songwriters, at least one songwriter must have contributed to each song as a co-writer.

There are potential disadvantages to registering a collection that you should understand. In theory, a song collection, as opposed to each individual song in that collection, is only protected by copyright to the extent that there has been sufficient originality in the selection and arrangement of the songs put together as one "work." If it's obvious that you randomly selected the songs with no apparent theme (such as by registering every song you've ever written under one copyright form or registering groups of songs that have no relationship to each other), theoretically the copyright in the collection could be challenged. If the validity of that copyright and its registration is later denied by a court, it's possible that you would no longer be able to use that registration as a source of evidence of the date of your authorship. In that case, all of the statutory advantages of registration would be lost for each individual song in the collection, and each song would only be protected as though it had never been registered for copyright at all. This is really a fairly obscure legal possibility, and I

In theory, a song collection, as opposed to each individual song in that collection, is only protected by copyright to the extent that there has been sufficient originality in the selection and arrangement of the songs put together as one "work."

know of no major cases on this subject, but when you register a collection, it's a good idea to use a title that implies at least some minimal overall concept (for example, *Songs of Love*; *Dance Tunes, Volume I*; *Songs from 1988*; *Ballads*; *Songs for Laura*; *The Best of (your name), Volume I*).

Another issue in registering multiple songs is the *indexing* of titles by the Copyright Office. This indexing procedure is one of the advantages of copyright registration, because it's legally deemed *public notice* of your registration (discussed below), and it makes searches of the copyright office records much easier (for example, to find the name of an author, a copyright owner, or the date of registration). A collective work will only be indexed by the title of the collection (not by individual song titles), unless you later file a CA registration form (a supplemental copyright form designed to correct or amplify a prior registration) listing all of the separate song titles that were registered as part of the collection. You should wait until the Copyright Office sends you a copy of your original PA registration form with a registration number and date, because in completing your CA form, you will have to refer to the number and registration date entered on the original PA form by the Copyright Office.

What Is the Effect of Registration?

Copyright registration only establishes a public record of your copyright claim. Many songwriters mistakenly believe that it firmly establishes their claim. For example, just because one writer of a jointly written song decides to register a copyright form PA without the names of the other writers doesn't mean the other writers do not still own equal shares of the copyright. The omitted writers should, however, for best protection, file a form CA to claim that a correction of the original PA form should be made, and that their names should be added to the basic registration.

Copyright registration is also usually necessary before any legal action for infringement can be initiated. If the registration is made within three months after publication of the song or, in the case of infringement of an unpublished song, prior to any infringement, and if the copyright owner wins an infringement case, the owner may be entitled to a court award of attorneys' fees and *statutory damages*. Otherwise, the copyright owner would be limited to only the *actual damages* suffered and the profits made by the person or company that infringed the copyright.

This can be an important legal advantage, because in many cases the infringer either hasn't made any profits from the infringement or has expenses that reduce the profits substantially. The concept of *statutory damages* allows the court to award damages that are "fair and just." Under the most recent revision to the copyright laws, a court can award statutory damages of up to $200 for an innocent infringement, $500 to $20,000 for an ordinary infringement, and up to $100,000 for a "willful" infringement.

> Copyright registration is also usually necessary before any legal action for infringement can be initiated.

An additional advantage of copyright registration is that it constitutes *constructive notice* to the public of the facts of your claim of authorship and ownership. This means that the public is deemed to have knowledge of your claim whether or not a particular person or company has searched the records of the Copyright Office. For example, if one of your collaborators for a particular song attempts to assign the entire song to a music publisher without your knowledge, your registration will enable you to "void" and nullify the transfer of your interest unless the publisher or collaborator can initially prove you did not co-write the song. Without the registration, it would be up to you to prove initially that you *did* co-write the song.

That brings up another advantage of registration—the legal *burden of proof* in court for copyright disputes. If copyright registration has been made either before legal publication or within five years after publication, it constitutes "prima facie" evidence of the facts in the registration. This means that someone contesting a registration, whether an accused infringer or otherwise, has the initial burden to introduce sufficient evidence to prove the registration is invalid, by either establishing that: (a) the registering owner did not properly obtain ownership from the author or a prior owner; (b) the author did not create the song; (c) the song was copied from another source; or (d) the song was otherwise not an original work of authorship. The registering owner has no burden to prove anything until the opposing party has produced such evidence.

From this discussion, you should see why registration of your song in the Copyright Office of the Library of Congress is by far the best registration and protection. There are independent registration services (such as that offered by the National Academy of Songwriters in Los Angeles), but they should be used only for short-term purposes, for example, to offer some formal evidence of protection when you may be ready to present your song to someone but haven't had time to register a copyright in Washington, D.C.

Independent registration services, if they are reliable and efficient, *do* provide an independent source of evidence of your claim of creation on or before the date of registration, but they provide none of the important statutory advantages discussed in this section. It is also important to remember that, as with copyright registration, registration with independent services does *not* establish your claim—it just provides a dated record of the claim.

Do-it-yourself methods, such as sending a self-addressed letter in the mail, are virtually worthless and should never be used to protect your songs. When in doubt, do it the right way: File a copyright registration form with the Copyright Office!

What About Copyright Notice?

Under present law for published works, a notice on all "visually perceptible copies" (for example, lead sheets, other sheet music, demo tapes, records), in "such manner and location as to give reasonable notice of the claim or copyright," is still required to obtain the maximum benefit of copyright protection. The proper copyright notice is either a *C* in a circle or the word "Copyright," followed by the year of first publication and the name of the copyright owner. The omission of any element of that notice results in an incorrect notice, having the same legal effect as if there were no copyright notice at all.

Always remember that the proper copyright notice date is *not* the date of creation, and it's *not* the date of registration. As you learned earlier in this chapter, the date of publication has a specific legal meaning. No copyright notice is technically required for unpublished works. The Copyright Office, however, recommends that to avoid inadvertent publication without notice, a notice such as "Unpublished Work Copyright 1989 John Doe" should be placed on any copies or phonorecords that leave the possession and control of the creator. Until legal publication has occurred, *you can continue to update your unpublished copyright notice*. That means if you're positive your song hasn't been published, you will not have to send tapes with copyright notices that make it appear you're promoting an old song! (Be careful, however. As I discussed earlier, the dividing line between preliminary distribution and legal publication is sometimes difficult to determine. Therefore, if you believe publication may have occurred for a particular song, continue to use the same year in all of your copyright notices.)

As I've already mentioned, in previous versions of the copyright laws, under certain circumstances, the publication of a work without copyright notice could have resulted in that work being in the public domain, free to be used by anyone forever without penalty. Under present law, however, revised to bring the United States in line with the requirements of the Berne Convention, publication without notice cannot invalidate your copyright and put your song in the public domain under any circumstances. Despite that safeguard, it's important you realize that infringers who innocently rely on an authorized copy or a phonorecord without a copyright notice may be found by a court to have no liability whatsoever for the infringement if they prove they were misled by the omission of notice. So without a proper copyright notice, your work could still be used by someone without payment!

Make it a habit to place the correct copyright notice on all lead sheets and demo tapes of your songs. The rights you protect and save may be your own!

International Copyright Protection

Copyright protection for your songs in foreign countries can be a complex issue, as there is no international copyright law that applies everywhere. Protection in a particular country depends solely upon the laws of that country.

Countries offering the best protection to U.S. songwriters are usually those having agreed to particular copyright treaties or conventions. These include countries with private, direct, bilateral treaties with the U.S. and countries that have joined a major, multi-country copyright *convention* to which we also belong.

The United States is now a member of both the Berne Convention and the Universal Copyright Convention, the two most widely accepted international copyright treaties. Under both treaties, as a general rule, a song written at least partially by a U.S. citizen or other person who normally lives in the United States is entitled to protection in each member country in accordance with the same copyright laws that would protect the works of that country's own citizens. Under the Berne Convention, such protection is also offered to any song first published in a Berne member country on or after March 1, 1989. The Berne Convention provides additional protection by virtue of minimum standards established uniformly for all of its member countries.

Most major foreign countries that commonly exploit songs and records of U.S. artists and songwriters are members with us under either Berne or the UCC (for example, Canada, Japan, Australia, and most countries in western Europe). If you are concerned about the protection of your songs in a particular distant foreign country, however, the Copyright Office recommends that you investigate the extent of protection of foreign works in that country *before publication anywhere*, because protection in that country may depend upon certain facts about your registration, copyright status, or form of publication *only at the time of first publication*.

Until legal publication has occurred, you can continue to update your unpublished copyright notice. That means if you're positive your song hasn't been published, you will not have to send tapes with copyright notices that make it appear you're promoting an old song!

If the complicated information in this chapter hasn't either put you to sleep or prompted you to paper-train your dog with the rest of this book, you're on your way! Just remember that, although I've covered a variety of specific topics concerning copyrights in this chapter (and further copyright issues will arise in other chapters), the treatment of copyright in this book is just a broad overview of an extremely technical and complex area. There are various qualifications and exceptions to many of the general rules discussed here. If you want more specific information concerning copyrights, contact either a copyright attorney or the Copyright Office, Library of Congress, Washington, D.C. 20559. Request a copy of their current list of application forms, regulations, and circulars. These materials explain registration and protection in much greater detail.

CHAPTER 2

LEGAL LIMITS TO CREATING SONGS AND DEMOS

So now you've read and understood chapter one, and you think you know how to stay out of trouble. Don't be so confident! There are may other ways you might violate someone's legal rights when you create a song or demo.

Many of you probably think it's safe to write a parody of a hit song, because Weird Al Yankovic has done it frequently over the years, and you've heard hundreds of different parodies on Dr. Demento's radio show. You probably also believe you can write a song anytime about your favorite movie star—a tribute like "Bette Davis Eyes." When you produce your demos, you feel sure you can take a rhythm guitar track from a hit ten years ago and use it in your latest song, because you hear records on the radio every day that use samples of sounds from other records!

Ignorance might be bliss, but it can also be dangerous! None of the uses I've described above are totally permissible without major restrictions and qualifications.

Parody and Satire

The copyright law, as interpreted by the courts, allows some uses of otherwise protected material to be considered fair uses (certain uses of songs for criticism, comment, news reporting, teaching, scholarship, or research) and therefore permissible without any payment or obligation to the copyright owner. The majority of these involve uses of an entire song, not the creation of a song, so I will not discuss them here.

In many circumstances, parody and satire may also be fair uses, as our society has long favored these forms of expression as part of our cherished right of free speech. Throughout musical history, songs ranging from Christmas carols to contemporary hits have been copied for humorous reasons. Weird Al Yankovic has on occasion been one of the most visible and popular satirists with parody songs like his early 1980s version of Michael Jackson's "Beat It" called "Eat It."

Songwriters should be aware of the limitations in this area, however, because all parodies and satirical versions of protected songs will not automatically be considered a fair use. In fact, because of the risks in this area of the law, successful songwriters of parodies like Yankovic will usually obtain permission before creating their humorous versions of hit songs. In the mid-1980s, Rick Dees, a Los Angeles disc jockey, was sued for his unauthorized parody of "When Sunny Gets Blue" called "When Sunny Sniffs Glue." He won his case, but the court did not merely dispense with the issue based on the fact that his use was only a parody. They applied specific legal tests to determine whether his parody was legally allowable.

The most critical factors a court would likely examine in deciding whether a song parody is a fair use include:

1. *The nature of the parody.* Some legal decisions have held that the song being substantially copied for a parody must be at least partially the object of the parody (although other courts have rejected this requirement). So if you plan to take the music from a popular song about a love affair and write your own lyrics satirizing your city's inept baseball team, you should first obtain permission from the copyright owner.

2. *The amount of the original song that is used.* Generally, a parody (without permission) may only use enough of the original work to "recall or conjure up" the "object" of the satire. Part of the reasoning for this rule is that a parody should not substantially affect the market for the original song. If a parody is too similar in sound or lyric, a court might find that the demand for the original version has been adversely affected.

All parodies and satirical versions of protected songs will not automatically be considered a fair use.

Therefore, even though some cases appear to allow a very substantial portion of the original song to be used in a parody, a satirical version that changes only a few words or phrases of the original song would not likely be considered a fair use. The imprecise application of this rule might explain why a successful satirist like Weird Al Yankovic normally obtains permission to create his parodies, because he generally uses all of the music from the original song, even duplicating the production sound.

Laws outside the area of copyright may also be used to stop a parody version. For example, normal obscenity laws apply to parodies. If a satirical version of a song is found legally obscene in a particular jurisdiction, the fact that it is a parody will not save the songwriter from legal liability.

Parodies are subject to laws of defamation and disparagement, as we'll see in the next section. If your song will be satirizing an identifiable person, company, product, or service, ask an attorney if the lyrics might cause potential legal problems.

Defamation

Laws of defamation include such commonly heard terms as *libel* and *slander*, which only refer to the different forms by which defamatory comments are communicated (for example, orally or in writing). The distinction is not important to this discussion.

The subject of defamation could fill an entire book in itself, because there are countless statutes and cases, both on national and state levels, that govern this area of the law. For songwriters, it's important to understand only the most basic principles.

When you write song lyrics that mention a particular, identifiable person or company, or a product or service of a person or company, you must be extremely careful. If those lyrics are false and have a "tendency" to injure the personal, professional, or business reputation of that person or company, or the products or services of that person or company, you could be liable for defamation.

An example of lyrics that might defame a particular person would be those claiming that person is a drug addict, an alcoholic, or a thief. Defamation of a product might be found where a song lyric claims a product caused some harm to the singer or a character in the song. For example, you should not write a song in which someone commits suicide after drinking a particular brand of tequila.

To illustrate how sensitive some companies are to "commercial disparagement," in 1988 the company that operates Welcome Wagon sued the producers of the motion picture *Big* for defamation based upon one comic line in that movie. A group of male employees was making suggestive comments in a scene about an overly friendly, seductively dressed female employee. One stated, "She's the company welcome wagon." The executives of Welcome Wagon believed that the comment injured the reputation of their representatives by making the public think they are sexually promiscuous!

The vast majority of songs that are exposed in the commercial market do not enter the area of possible defamation. If you write some form of story song about real people, companies, or products, however, or if you casually use identifiable names in any negative way, you might have a problem. If you have any doubts about lyrics that will mention a particular person, company, product, or service, get legal advice.

Rights of Publicity

This is another area of the law that could fill a volume in itself. In general, the legal principle involved prevents the unauthorized use of a person's name, picture, voice, or *likeness* for commercial purposes. I'll discuss the application of these laws to sampling later, but for the purposes of songwriting alone (before production of a demo), we're only concerned with the relationship of the law to the use of names.

A significant complexity in this area is that the *right of publicity* has not been established as a matter of federal law but is given individual treatment in a number of states. In fact, one important aspect of these laws — the right of heirs of a deceased entertainer to enforce a right of publicity after death — has been handled by different courts and state legislatures inconsistently. It might be legal to use the name of Janis Joplin or Jimi Hendrix in some states but be subject to legal actions in others.

Unlike defamation laws, the right of publicity has nothing to do with truth, falsity, or injury to reputation. The simple use of a name in your song can be illegal. Don't assume that the star or other public person you want to mention will be flattered by your song, because many celebrities are extremely sensitive to the constant overexposure their names and lives receive in the media. For the classic hit "Bette Davis Eyes" (performed by Kim Carnes), the songwriters obtained that star's permission for the

Unlike defamation laws, the right of publicity has nothing to do with truth, falsity, or injury to reputation. The simple use of a name in your song can be illegal.

use of her name. If you plan to use the names of celebrities or other persons in your song, be safe and ask their approval of your intended use.

Sampling and Processing

Under current legal principles, as long as you do not take a substantial portion of any element of a song protected by copyright, you can attempt to imitate a particular musical or instrumental sound or style with no fear of penalty. As you'll see later in this section, however, you are not on such apparently safe ground if you imitate someone's vocal style.

With rapid technological advances in digital recording devices and keyboards in recent years, most songwriters are no longer content with mere imitation. Anyone who is financially able can now purchase or rent equipment that can *sample* and identically reproduce virtually any sound known to man, whether vocal, instrumental, or otherwise. Names such as Emulator, Synclavier, Fairlight, Mirage, and Kurzweil have become synonymous with these techniques, and the practice has become so widespread that there are "user groups" that trade discs containing a variety of sounds.

> A melody line is one of the most protectible elements of a song copyright.

After I had heard that discs duplicating various sounds and voices of star artists and musicians were being copied and circulated, I realized that some portion of a chapter in this book should discuss what legal limits might exist on this new technique for copying the unique artistic creations of others. If you've always wanted to make a demo using the sound of Eddie Van Halen's guitar, Phil Collins's drums, or the distinctive voices of Barbara Streisand or Bobby McFerrin, this knowledge should save some of you the eventual cost and embarrassment of a lawsuit.

The kind of sampling that blatantly takes a substantial part of a melody line, instrumental solo, or other musical or vocal performance from a prior recording is too obvious to merit much discussion here. A melody line is one of the most protectible elements of a song copyright, and a sound recording copyright can be readily used to protect against the sampling of a substantial part of any musical or vocal performance from a particular recording. As I've already mentioned and will discuss again later, judges and juries decide whether the amount taken from one song or sound recording for another song or sound recording is substantial enough to impose liability for copyright infringement.

Despite what you may hear on many "rap" and dance records today, don't believe for a moment that record companies and music publishers are not actively protecting their rights and insisting upon payment for the sampling of substantial, readily identifiable guitar, synthesizer, or other musical or vocal lines that are used intact in new recordings. One rap group I represented took an entire melody line from the theme song of a television program popular in the early 1970s! The record was released by a major label before either I or any attorney for the label was aware of that sample. The music publisher agreed not to sue for copyright infringement on the condition that the *entire* copyright for the rap group's song be assigned to that company. In another case, a record producer for an independent label sampled a distinctive guitar part from the theme song to a motion picture popular in the 1960s. The record company owning the master recording of the theme song agreed to charge a certain number of cents per copy sold for the use of the guitar part, substantially reducing the money earned by the songwriters of the new song.

This entire area is one of some ignorance to many songwriters who are newly discovering the joys of sampling. The penalties for disregarding these laws can be severe. The normal damages for copyright infringement are the infringer's profits. So a court could conceivably order that *all* of the money earned from an infringing song be paid to the owner of the copyright in the original work. Additionally, statutory damages of up to $100,000 can be awarded for willful copyright infringement.

Aside from these obvious areas of copyright infringement, the issue I'm primarily concerned with here is the taking of *isolated* sounds from a rhythm track, or groove, or a distinctive instrumental or vocal performance on a record. I believe this will likely become the next area for enforcement of legal rights against sampling.

The majority of you—those who use sampling only for demos—will probably not face legal problems. It's extremely rare for anyone to be interested in suing a songwriter based upon a mere song demo. Often, however, a song demo might be so effectively produced that the producer of the eventual master recording cannot duplicate the "feel" of the demo or some particular sounds on the demo that would make the record better. In those situations, a songwriter might be asked to bring computer discs or other actual recorded tracks to the studio to be used in the production of the master recording. It's possible, then, that *a record might make it onto the airwaves and into the record stores with sounds a songwriter has sampled from someone else for an initial demo.*

As a practical matter, any sound, instrument, or voice you have sampled that has then been processed or manipulated into another sound totally unrecognizable from the original sound or "nominal pitch" is probably fair game. As long as you don't reveal the source of your new sound to anyone, it would be unlikely that anyone would recognize the creation or performance you copied. Be aware, though, that technology exists to compare sound waves or wave forms from two different sound recordings and conclusively prove that a particular sound was duplicated from another recording, no matter how different the processed sound is to the naked ear!

What if someone proves you sampled particular sounds or musical or vocal performances, and the final sounds you used are clearly identical to the sounds or performances you sampled? Who has legal rights against you and under what circumstances?

This discussion is intended only as a review of some laws and legal principles that *may* be applied to the sampling of individual sounds in the future. It is not a complete or final treatment of the possibilities, however, because as this is written: (a) many of these issues have not been resolved in the courts and are not covered sufficiently in current laws; and (b) such a discussion would be far too complex and technical for this book and would give you a splitting headache.

Copyright Law

As I've already discussed, this is the major body of law that protects the unauthorized copying and use of the original creations of others. For the copyright issues raised by sampling, two key questions arise: (a) whether the "work" being copied is original enough to be protected by copyright; and (b) if the "work" being copied is protected by copyright, whether there is substantial similarity between the protected work and

---

The normal damages for copyright infringement are the infringer's profits. So a court could conceivably order that *all* of the money earned from an infringing song be paid to the owner of the copyright in the original work.

the copier's work. (As most sampling involves the use of sounds and performances from records and tapes widely sold to the public, I'm ignoring the issue of access to the copyrighted work, another key element in proving infringement mentioned in chapter one.)

There are four categories of potential copyright owners whose rights you may be theoretically violating when you sample sounds from an existing recording:

1. songwriters and music publishers, who may own all or part of the copyright in the musical composition from which the sound was taken;

2. singers and instrumentalists, who some legal theorists believe may be entitled to claim copyright in any performances possessing a sufficient degree of originality, although these types of copyrights have not really been claimed or utilized in the past;

3. record producers, who are not mentioned specifically in the Copyright Law, but were identified in committee reports when Congress was deliberating over the Copyright Act of 1976, and who were viewed as potential copyright claimants based upon the originality and creativity inherent in the capturing and electronic processing of sounds and the compiling and editing of sounds to make the final sound recordings; and

4. record companies and others who own copyrights for the actual sound recordings on which the sampled sounds were originally recorded.

Regardless of the category of potential copyright claimant, if a "work" is not considered an original work of authorship, there is no copyright protection whatsoever. Unfortunately, it's not always easy to determine which elements of a song or sound recording will be deemed sufficient in themselves to constitute an original work for copyright purposes.

The creation of one isolated sound would not likely merit copyright protection, although a collection of sounds recorded in a particular order might. For example, in a recording of a carpenter striking a nail, no original work of authorship has been created by the carpenter, but the sampling of that sound and its processing into a variety of sounds involving some degree of originality as to melody, pitch, or rhythm would probably be deemed original enough for copyright protection. In one 1983 case, a federal court ruled that the extensive editing and compilation of sounds of a hockey game (for purposes of a video game) were sufficiently original for copyright protection, although the mere recording of such sounds, with nothing added, would not have been.

Generally, as mentioned earlier, most courts have determined that copyrights in musical compositions cover mostly the originality in creation of the melody line and lyrics. As to the rights of either the songwriter or music publisher of a particular song, then, there would be no copyright infringement in the copying of a particular synthesizer sound or other instrument or voice, so long as there is no substantial copying or use of the melody line or lyrics (the issue of substantial similarity, of course, applies to all forms of copying).

As to the singer or other performer of a musical composition, the late Melville Nimmer, perhaps our country's foremost copyright authority, once noted that "there is little question but that a performer's rendition of a work written by another may by itself constitute an original work." No cases have yet attempted to apply this theory to copyright law, however, and, as a practical matter, two major factors make it an unlikely area for such an application.

First, any such copyright would derive from the copyright in the musical composition, requiring the permission of the songwriter or music publisher for recognition of the performance as a separately copyrightable, derivative work. Owners of major song copyrights are extremely careful in allowing others to own rights in derivative works, usually giving permission only for major projects and substantial payments. Second, most record company agreements with performers, whether vocal or musical artists, specify that all of the performers' efforts will be works made for hire, meaning that the employer will own any copyright that has been created by the performance. Don't overlook the discussion in the next two sections concerning unfair competition and rights of publicity, however, because those are the two most likely areas that performers will use to protect their rights.

The theoretical copyright envisioned by Congress for record producers, those responsible for "capturing and electronically processing the sounds, and compiling and editing them to make the final sound recording," is limited by the same two restrictions discussed in the previous paragraph. For this reason, as well as the lack of any major legal precedent on this issue, copyrights for record producers are seldom claimed and protected unless the producer has produced recordings apart from any record company and will be exploiting or promoting the recordings independently.

What about record companies or others who own master recordings? Without regard to the originality of the music or sounds recorded, and aside from the rights they possess through the services of others involved in either the performances or the capturing, processing, compiling, and editing of sounds, virtually any sound recording is legally protected under a separate sound recording copyright. This copyright *protects the actual sounds recorded on the record*. In the previously mentioned legal decision involving the video hockey game, the court also stated that a computer chip containing sounds also constitutes a sound recording protected by copyright.

> There is no certain, absolute number of notes, bars, or words that may be legally copied, and there is no finite, quantitative standard.

As a matter of common practice in the music industry thus far, record companies have not enforced their sound recording rights to punish those who sample isolated sounds. This is partly because, traditionally, record companies have been concerned mostly with record pirates who copy entire recordings and manufacture counterfeit or "bootleg" products, competing in the marketplace with the artist's legitimate products and reducing sales of the original recording. As I mentioned earlier, though, these companies have also begun to enforce their rights when any reasonably identifiable portion of a sound recording has been taken, because *record companies are extremely sensitive to anyone attempting to profit by using any element of the success they have created for their artist*. If you take something readily and obviously identifiable with a particular artist, you are treading on potentially sacred ground.

As a practical matter, it is probably unlikely, but not totally inconceivable, that Atlantic Records will initiate legal action against anyone who samples and processes a single sound of Phil Collins's snare drum, or that Arista Records will sue someone who takes one sound from Kenny G's saxophone, or that Elektra Records will become enraged over the sampling of a single note of Tracy Chapman's voice. Their action or inaction in these cases will likely depend upon *how* those isolated sounds are used. For example, although the taking of a few sounds might not otherwise be substantial enough to claim copyright infringement or the violation of any other legal right, what about the copying of a few identifiable sounds and the use of those sounds by repeating them continuously in another song? At present, that technique seems to have become widespread in the rap and dance music industry. For that type of use, the identity of the original song that was the source of the sound is probably obvious to the listener, and it's likely that by the time you read this, a court will have imposed liability against a producer, record company, or songwriter for that kind of copying.

At least as far as the copyright law goes, the second major reason record companies may not yet have been aggressive in pursuing those who sample single, isolated sounds is the law's requirement that substantial similarity exist between the original work and the copy in order to support a legal finding of infringement. Assuming you are copying something that is protected under copyright law by either a songwriter, music publisher, performer, producer, or record company, what is substantial copying? As I mentioned previously, there is no certain, absolute number of notes, bars, or words that may be legally copied, and there is no finite, quantitative standard.

Clearly, the most minimal copying of one, isolated sound of an instrument or voice from a sound recording would not constitute copyright infringement. Just as obviously, the sampling of an entire melody line would. Perhaps one day soon, the repetition of only one identifiable sound throughout an entire song will also be considered copyright infringement. Where will the line between permissible use and copyright infringement eventually be drawn for the sampling of individual sounds? Unfortunately, it's very unlikely there will ever be one concrete, easy-to-follow rule.

At present (and for the foreseeable future), courts use an *ordinary observer* test to determine what is a substantial "taking" of protected material sufficient for copyright infringement. Regardless of the testimony of legal experts that the similarity between two works is sufficient to infer that one work or sound was copied from the other, it is still up to a jury (or judge without a jury) to decide whether such copying took too much of the original work. (Remember also that in the case of songs that have not been widely sold or distributed, the creator might have difficulty proving that the copier had access to the original work. In the Bee Gees case mentioned earlier, this defective element of proof caused the judge to overrule a verdict in favor of the songwriter making the claim, despite the fact that the jury had found the two songs to be substantially similar.)

Right of Publicity

At least regarding the sampling of voices, this is a far more likely area of the law to be used to enforce the legal rights of performers. I discussed earlier that this legal principle prevents the unauthorized use of one's name, picture, voice, or *likeness* for commercial purposes and is given different levels of protection in different states.

California law, for example, specifically forbids the use of another's voice in any manner "on or in products, merchandise, or goods, or for purposes of advertising or selling, or soliciting purchases of, products, merchandise, goods or services . . ." The sampling of even one note of a singer's performance would appear to be covered by this legal principle.

Even though no legal cases involving sampling appear to have been initiated so far under these kinds of laws, another legal decision makes it appear likely that a court would quickly protect a recording artist in such a case. In 1988, a federal court ruled (at least under California law) that when a distinctive voice of a professional

Right of publicity prevents the unauthorized use of one's name, picture, voice, or *likeness* for commercial purposes and is given different levels of protection in different states.

singer is widely known and is deliberately imitated in order to sell a product, the seller of the product has taken a legitimate property right of the performing artist, and the performer has a legal right of action.

In that case, the Ford Motor Company had requested that Bette Midler perform her vocal version of "Do You Want to Dance?" for a proposed commercial. When she refused, Ford hired one of her former backup singers to closely imitate Midler's vocal style. Although an actual trial of the case has not yet been held, and the final issue of legal liability has not yet been determined, the court's decision established that such a right of legal action exists (at least in California) and enabled Midler to proceed with her claim against Ford. Singer Tom Waits recently filed a legal action based upon a similar claim against an advertiser who hired a singer to imitate his style. *If courts and famous performers are protecting against the imitation of a famous vocal style to sell unrelated products, it's inevitable that they will also protect against the actual copying of the sound of a famous vocalist to sell a record.*

To date, the sampling of one note or sound created by a musician or programmer, even if performed in a distinctive style unmistakably associated with that person, does not appear to be covered under any right of publicity laws now written and has not been the subject of any major legal action. This is possibly because the term *likeness* (the only term in such laws potentially capable of such broad interpretation) has generally referred only to the "image" of the person. From reading this discussion, however, it should be clear to you that artists (whether vocal or musical), are becoming more and more sensitive to this issue. So it appears likely that the protection of laws like these will continue to be expanded.

Unfair Competition

The Lanham Act is a federal law that provides various rules regulating certain business and commercial practices. A complete discussion could fill volumes in itself. For our purposes, it's important to know that one of its legal principles is that the commercial activities of one business may not unfairly compete with the activities of another.

A common claim of *unfair competition* is that one person or company is selling goods or merchandise that either: (a) so closely resembles the goods or merchandise of another person or company that it appears that the imitator is "passing off" their product as the product of someone else; or (b) imitates another product so closely as to unfairly compete with that product. Almost all copyright infringement or right of publicity claims in the area of sampling can be expected to include a claim of unfair competition. So even if you think you know how to avoid the other two areas of the law, there may be a third kind of legal protection used to punish you!

How can you be safe if you're going to sample something? The best bet is to restrict your sampling to song demos only. If you're going to use a sample on an actual record that will be released, process the sound beyond recognition and tell no one the source you sampled. Otherwise, if any readily identifiable sound from an easily recognizable source is used in any significant manner on a popular record, you will likely face a lawsuit from a publisher, record company, or recording artist.

How can you be safe if you're going to sample something? The best bet is to restrict your sampling to song demos only.

CHAPTER 3

LEGAL PROBLEMS WITH CO-WRITERS

It's critically important to understand how your rights to a song are affected when you write with other songwriters, because the majority of hit songs are written by more than one person, and it's likely you will have to collaborate with someone at some point in your career. This is a very common area of difficulty and disagreement between songwriters, because most co-writers do not understand their rights and obligations in these situations. It doesn't matter whether you've written a song with your sister, your wife, or your best friend. A lack of knowledge of these issues can cause you a lot of pain later, and if your song becomes a major hit, it may also cost you a lot of money.

Co-Writer Situations

To realize how easy it is to misunderstand the legal rights of collaborators, let's look at some hypothetical situations. Imagine that you finally get together with a songwriter you've been wanting to work with. You bounce a few ideas back and forth. Impressed with each other, you decide to write a few songs. You record simple piano-vocal demos of the songs on a portable cassette recorder. Over the next few months, these problems arise:

1. For the first song, you wrote all of the music and one-half of the lyrics. The two of you decide to license the song for a motion picture for a $1000 synchronization fee. Do you automatically get $750?

2. For the second song, you wrote only the music, and your collaborator wrote only the lyrics. After promoting the song for a few months to music publishers, producers, and recording artists, all of the criticism is the same—your music is wonderful, but your collaborator's lyrics are terrible. You decide to find another lyricist to rewrite all of the lyrics without your original collaborator's approval. Can you create a new song with your music and another songwriter's lyrics without owing the original lyricist any of the money earned from the new song?

3. The third song you wrote together is perfect for a demo tape featuring you and your band. After promoting this tape for a few months, you get interest from two major record companies that want to sign your group. Both labels insist that the co-written song is by far your biggest potential hit and will be the first single they will release after you're signed. Your collaborator, who is not in your group and who desperately needs money to pay the rent, finds an advertis-

ing agency willing to pay $10,000 because they think the song is perfect for a national advertising campaign for a deodorant spray they represent. You tell the record companies about your collaborator's plans, and they insist they will not sign your group if the song is used in the commercial. Can you prevent your collaborator from giving a license to the advertising agency, or can you otherwise stop the agency from using the song?

4. Your diligent promotional efforts for the fourth song have paid off, and you finally receive the call you've been waiting for. Sally Superstar's producer loves the song and wants to put it on her next album. Your timing was perfect, because every other song on the album is finished and the producer was waiting for a "killer ballad" like yours to finish the project. The record company wants to release the album soon, so Sally and her producer, Eddie Ears, need to begin recording the song within the next five days. Eddie, like many record producers who like to own rights to songs, insists that you assign all of the music publishing rights in your song to his company as a condition of having it recorded on Sally's album. Your collaborator is camping somewhere in Montana and can't be reached. Can you assign all music publishing rights in the song to the producer?

Unfortunately for you, and surprising as it may seem, the answer to all of the questions above is "No!" Now you can understand why the legal effects of collaboration are some of the most misunderstood aspects of the business of songwriting. Hopefully, this chapter will clear up some of the confusion.

How Is a Joint Work Created?

A *joint work* under the Copyright Law, is a "work prepared by two or more authors with the intention that their contributions be merged into inseparable or interdependent parts of a unitary whole." As I discussed in chapter one, a song is subject to copyright protection when "fixed in any tangible medium of expression . . . from which [it] can be perceived, reproduced or otherwise communicated, either directly or with the aid of a machine or device."

That formal legal definition means that when you create lyrics or music, intending that someday they will be part of a song, your creation becomes part of a joint work when it is recorded on tape or written on a lead sheet along with someone else's lyrics or music. Even though your individual contribution might have been separately protected under the copyright law and suitable for copyright registration by itself, the song that results from the *merging* of the individual contributions of the songwriters is then covered by the copyright laws in its joint form, *regardless of whether the complete song has been registered in Washington, D.C.* (As I mentioned in chapter one, remember that registration is still advisable to provide evidence of your claim to authorship of the song, as well as to give you certain legal advantages if you sue someone for infringement.)

You don't have to be physically present when the merging of creations occurs, as long as you have approved the merging of creative contributions. In fact, it's not even necessary that you knew who your eventual collaborator would be when you composed your music or wrote your lyrics!

A *joint work* is a "work prepared by two or more authors with the intention that their contributions be merged into inseparable or interdependent parts of a unitary whole."

Your "approval" of creative contributions does *not* have to be in writing and can be implied from the circumstances of the collaboration. For example, if you submit your lyrics to composers and ask them to create music for the song, and if you allow them to record a demo tape of their version and promote it to publishers for a few weeks, that would likely be considered a sufficient merging of your lyrics and the composer's music to create a joint work.

Great. You now have an intentional or unintentional business partner for your song!

What Rights Does Each Songwriter Have to the Song?

1. *Collaborators each own undivided, equal interests in the whole song.* Unless they agree to some other division of ownership and income participation, two co-writers each own one-half of the song, three co-writers each own one-third, etc. These fractional interests apply to the *entire* song, and separate lyrical and musical ownership rights to jointly created songs do not exist without a written agreement among the songwriters.

   What about songwriters who only make a minimal creative contribution? There are legal cases that appear to protect the primary writers of a song from the ownership claims of those who make only minor contributions to its overall creation. The writing of a few words or composing of a few notes will not normally entitle that songwriter to an equal share, even without an agreement. The same rule applies to any other contribution that would not be suitable for separate copyright protection (such as some chord changes or vocal harmonies). The most common example is the title. Many songwriters ask if they need to share their copyright with a friend who suggested the title. In all fairness, perhaps you should pay the person who thought up the title, but there is no legal requirement that they own any portion of the copyright.

   Collaboration ownership problems can arise frequently in studio sessions, where a producer, musician, or singer makes a suggestion for a small change in the melody line or lyrics or revises the chord structure, the harmonies, or the overall arrangement for the song. Often that person will think they now own a share of the song, but you cannot be forced to accept new co-owners of your song this way.

   If you've already completed a song before you start recording in the studio, and if the song has been previously fixed in a tangible medium of expression (whether or not it has been registered for copyright), and if you control the copyright to the song, any changes to that song can only be made with your permission. This is because technically the changes are creating a song derived from your original song, and the right to create derivative works, as I mentioned in chapter one, belongs to the copyright owners. You can therefore reject any changes you don't want. If you keep any significant creative contributions that have been made to your song by other people, however, and if you promote or exploit your song in that form, you have likely *consented* to the creation of a new joint work. You have therefore also consented to new joint owners of your copyright. If changes made to your song in the studio by other people are insignificant, you can either reject or use the changes as you wish, without

Separate lyrical and musical ownership rights to jointly created songs do not exist without a written agreement among the songwriters.

giving anyone else extra compensation or ownership rights (although you risk losing valuable friends, producers, singers, or musicians by taking *any* creative contribution without their agreement).

If your song is being fixed in a tangible medium of expression for the first time in a studio session, that's a much more risky situation. Participants who add minimal contributions will still not be entitled to ownership rights, but the line between sufficient and insufficient contributions is not always clear. If you have the slightest doubt as to what is being created and who will claim an ownership share, it's better to be cautious. You are now creating the "work" that will be protected by copyright, so make it clear to any potential creative contributor exactly what his or her financial and ownership interest in the song will be (if any at all).

2. *Contributions to a joint work cannot be separated.* This is often a source of conflict. Without the consent of the other songwriter involved, one writer can't simply remove that writer's contribution and get a new collaborator to replace it, because the original writer will still own one half of the new version (where there were only two writers of the original version). The ownership share of the original collaborator may not be reduced by the addition of new writers without consent. (It is important to note here that this legal prohibition is removed in almost all music publishing agreements unless you specifically require contrary language. See the discussion about single song agreements in chapter six.)

Again, the concept is of derivative works. For example, suppose a popular hit song is used for a beer commercial, but the lyrics have been totally rewritten to suit the product. The original lyricist is still entitled to a fifty percent share of the money received for that use of the song.

The theme from the television show *M*A*S*H* was originally written for a scene in the theatrical motion picture of the same name. Even though the song is commonly known as the "Theme from M*A*S*H," the original title was "Suicide is Painless," and there are lyrics originally written for the song that are sung in the motion picture version. Naturally, lyrics about suicide were not thought to be appropriate for the opening title theme of a prime-time television program, so the lyrics have never been used in connection with the TV show. Nonetheless, the lyricist has made a small fortune from small performing rights payments for the song's performance on prime-time network television and in the national syndication of the show to local television stations.

3. *Each co-writer can grant nonexclusive licenses without the consent of the other writers. Nonexclusive licenses* are permissions for use of a song that are not exclusively transferred to the person being given the license. For example, most synchronization licenses for the use of a song in a motion picture or television program are nonexclusive, because the owner of the copyright usually reserves the right to license the use of the song to some other television or motion picture producer. This is not always the case, however, as a television producer may be paying for the right to use the song as the theme song of a continuing series. In that situation, the license may indeed be an exclusive assignment of synchronization rights to the song.

The type of nonexclusive license described above should not be confused with a situation where a television or motion picture producer has required a complete assignment of music publishing ownership and control as a condition of using a song in the motion picture or television program. That type of agreement is an *exclusive* assignment of *all* rights to the song (which I'll discuss soon) and must be signed by all of the collaborators. After that type of agreement has been signed, the motion picture or television producer has total, exclusive control over the song. That's one of the reasons many such producers insist on owning music publishing rights.

Other than synchronization licenses, the most typical nonexclusive license is a *mechanical license* (for the mechanical reproduction of a song on recorded products like tapes and compact discs). Any disagreement between collaborators regarding a mechanical license can only arise for the *first* mechanical license for a song, because later mechanical licenses are *compulsory*, and even if all of the joint copyright owners of a song agree, they cannot refuse a request for that type of license (this was discussed in chapter one).

Problems between collaborators concerning nonexclusive licenses usually occur when the co-writers have different motivations for writing a song or when they simply disagree as to the best use of a song at a particular time. The third hypothetical situation at the beginning of this chapter is a good example of a writer who has co-written a song for a specific purpose without making sure the co-writer agreed with that purpose. Other disagreements may arise when multiple offers are received for the same song at the same time. Is it best for a song to be first used in a key scene of a major motion picture with major stars, even if there is no guarantee of a soundtrack album? Is it better for the song to be the first single on an album by a new act signed to a major label? Each writer may feel differently about the prospects for success of various projects.

For most recordings of songs by artists signed to major labels (except in a compulsory licensing situation, where other versions of the song have previously been recorded), the label, the artist, or the producer may want a guarantee that no other use of the song will be permitted until after the record has been released. Occasionally a song may be "hot" enough that an artist will want to record it despite the fact that some other artist will be recording and releasing it at the same time. Usually, however, the prospect of a competing recording will "kill" the deal, so a disagreement between collaborators as to competing recordings can be critical.

Now that I've given you some possible situations to worry about, I'll tell you that the majority of synchronization and mechanical licenses cause no dispute between collaborators at all. This is because very few songs initially attract multiple offers from different motion picture, television, and record producers at the same time. Usually, all of the songwriters are so pleased to have anyone interested in paying to use their song, they can hardly wait to sign the necessary paperwork!

Also, as a practical matter, one songwriter may not find it easy to grant a license against the wishes of the other co-writers. As to both synchronization and mechanical licenses, many users of music want the signatures of all of the songwriters. This is because they don't want any later dispute by the other

Any disagreement between collaborators regarding a mechanical license can only arise for the *first* mechanical license for a song, because later mechanical licenses are *compulsory*, and even if all of the joint copyright owners of a song agree, they cannot refuse a request for that type of license.

copyright owners regarding the license, and because the laws of many foreign countries require that any license to exploit a copyrighted work in their territory must be by permission of all copyright owners of the work. Don't rely on this for protection of your interests, though, because there are companies that *will* accept a license signed by one collaborator.

4. *No writer may assign an exclusive right to a song without the consent of the other writers.* Most importantly, this means that none of the co-writers can deal with the *publishing rights* (that is, the ownership and administration rights) of the other songwriters.

Other exclusive transfers of rights to the entire song are also forbidden. For example, no single collaborator can grant to one print music company the exclusive right to print sheet music of the song or grant to a subpublisher in France the exclusive administration rights to the song throughout Europe.

It is quite common, of course, for one songwriter to assign only his or her share of general music publishing rights, giving a particular publisher the same fractional interest in the entire song that the songwriter possessed before transferring the music publishing rights. So one of two equal co-writers could assign a 50 percent interest in the music publishing rights to one publisher. That publisher would then be a *co-publisher* or *co-administrator* with the remaining co-writer (or any music publishing company to which that co-writer may have given the remaining 50 percent share).

The rule forbidding exclusive assignments by less than all of the songwriters can become a special problem in two common circumstances: (a) where a collaborating songwriter, either through frequent travel, lack of interest, or numerous changes of address is generally unavailable to sign any paperwork concerning a proposed agreement that will include an exclusive assignment; and (b) where a collaborator, whether living far from the mainstream of music industry activity or not, has no understanding of the types of agreements that are necessary to promote and exploit songs and is generally unreceptive to any proposal from the "active" songwriters who are in the industry every day trying to generate interest in the song.

This is all complicated further by another important rule applying to exclusive transfers of rights in a copyright: No assignment of exclusive rights is valid unless made in writing. Oral agreements among the songwriting collaborators or between co-writers and an outside party are therefore unenforceable. So if you're the one seeking the right to make deals freely for a song, don't merely accept your collaborator's verbal assurance that it's all right. Most publishers, record producers, and others who may want certain exclusive rights will still insist upon the signature of all of the songwriters involved. Otherwise, your collaborator can have a change of heart and invalidate the transfer of rights as to that person's share of the song.

5. *All writers of a particular song have a legal duty to account to each other for any monies earned from any use or exploitation of the song.* In its most basic sense, this just means each writer has to pay the others their equal share of monies received, but the "receiving" writer should also provide information about the source of the monies and a copy of any accounting statement received by that writer along with the payment.

No assignment of exclusive rights is valid unless made in writing. Oral agreements among the songwriting collaborators or between co-writers and an outside party are therefore unenforceable.

6. *Each collaborating songwriter also has a legal duty to give credit to the other writers wherever a printed or visual credit appears for any of the writers.* This requirement is not contained in the copyright law but was imposed by one court in 1988 through an interpretation of the federal Lanham Act prohibition against *false designations* and representations of the *source* or *origin* of goods or services sold in interstate commerce. (Most states have similar laws that apply to goods or services sold within state boundaries.)

It had previously been clear only that songwriters have a legal right of action under the Lanham Act if authorship of their song were falsely attributed to someone who did not write the song and if *all* of their names were omitted from credit for that song. A 1988 Federal Circuit Court of Appeals case in California, however, held that a printed songwriting credit is also a false designation of origin when it attributes authorship to only one of several co-authors.

How Can Collaborators Protect Their Rights?

From the previous discussion, you can see that there are many different legal issues that may become important in the collaboration for a particular song, so each situation requires a different approach. The first thing to avoid is unnecessary paranoia at the beginning of a songwriting collaboration. You will probably never collaborate with anyone again if you make each writer sign a lengthy agreement before you even begin to write. So (getting away from the legal aspects of songwriting for, unfortunately, only a brief moment), make sure the collaboration is comfortable, and that you are likely to be completing a song together before you worry about any form of collaboration agreement.

As to those people with whom you don't want to collaborate, however, there may indeed be cause for concern and a preliminary, brief agreement. For example, prior to the start of a recording session where a song is being put in tangible form for the first time, it would be a good idea to have any producers, singers, or musicians sign a short release form. The form would basically contain information about the names of the songs for which they will be rendering their services, the money they will be paid, and a paragraph stating that any creative contributions or other results or proceeds of their services will belong solely to you with no further obligation for payment. With that kind of written provision, the nature and extent of their contribution to your session will not matter. You and your original co-writers will own and control the final song and master recording.

Be careful if you and your co-writers are members of a band that will be the primary performers (both for recording purposes and live performances) of songs you've co-written specifically for the band. For the non-songwriting members of the band, a release agreement such as the one I've just described may be considered insulting and may create conflict that will destroy the group.

Some bands have agreements under which all of the band members equally own and control the songs along with the songwriter members of the group. This is especially true in groups where the musicianship is a major factor in the marketability and success of the group's songs. In other bands, the songwriter members split equally the *songwriter's share* of income from the songs they write, while the entire band splits the income from the *publisher's share* and jointly controls the songs. Other groups leave song ownership, income, and control solely to the songwriter members. Regardless of the songwriter/non-songwriter makeup of your group, there is no single way in which this matter is always handled, and this is a sensitive issue to be resolved on a personal basis with your group.

Whether or not you're in a band, if you want to avoid any unfair application of the rule that all collaborators own equal shares of a song, the simplest solution would be a short written statement that "all right, title, and interest, including copyright, in and to the musical composition 'I Love You' will be owned as follows: John Jones — 75 percent; Susan Smith — 25 percent." It's important to understand that the percentages agreed upon between collaborators *do not affect control of the song*. For example, just because John Jones has 75 percent of the song doesn't mean that he has "majority rule" over decisions concerning nonexclusive licensing and exclusive assignments of rights. Susan Smith can still give a motion picture producer a nonexclusive license without John's approval, and John can assign only 75 percent of the administration rights of the song to a music publisher of his choice (he still needs Susan's written approval for assignment of her 25 percent share).

To protect yourself against being "stuck" with the creative contribution of a collaborator and continuing to owe your co-writer income even if you change the song and remove their contribution, a few tactics can be used. The easiest would be to orally agree that there will be no complete, merged song until you both consent.

Another general strategy might be suitable if you are the type of writer who writes lyrics alone and then looks for appropriate music, or if you generally write music alone and then look for appropriate lyrics. In either of these cases you might consider copyright registration of the lyrics alone or the music alone. The idea is to claim you have created a separately copyrightable work, with no intention that it will ever by merged with anyone else's work. You will then have a good argument that any song created after the date of that registration using your creation will be a derivative work. As I've already explained, a derivative work cannot be created at all without the consent of the copyright owner of the original song. This will prevent the possibility of any unintentional joint works that might be created when someone else's creative contribution merges with yours when the completed song is first put in tangible form.

The best way to employ the above technique for lyrics would be to use copyright registration Form TX, registering the work as poetry (if you register the words as song lyrics on a PA form, you will have obviously revealed your intention that someday your lyrics will be merged with someone else's music). For the separate registration of music, Form PA will still be appropriate. Regarding both strategies, however, be aware that if you *never* exploit lyrics or instrumental music alone, always eventually merging your music or lyrics with the lyrics or music of other songwriters, it might be difficult to prove that your original work was intended to stand on its own without further creative contributions.

A second strategy to avoid the problem of "inseparability" would be to agree in writing to a *reversion* of all rights to your contribution if the song is not used or exploited in a specific way within a certain period of time. (I will discuss this again later when I talk about music publishing agreements for a single song). For instance, you might agree that after one year, if no music publishing agreement acceptable to all of the writers is offered for the song, and if no other approved use of the song has occurred by that time, the writers may take back their individual creative contributions

> It's important to understand that the percentages agreed upon between collaborators do not affect control of the song.

to the song. This method should usually be used only where the contributions of different songwriters are very distinct (for example, where one has written only the lyrics and the other two have composed only the music). Otherwise, you'll get into a ridiculous argument over which musical measures or lyrical sentences belong to which writers.

What about collaborators' separate rights to grant nonexclusive licenses for use of a song without approval of other writers? Some writers simply agree that *no* license or agreement of any kind can be issued regarding a song without the approval of *all* of them. A common approach between songwriters of equal status is to recognize in an agreement that each of them can grant nonexclusive licenses without consulting the others, subject to certain protective requirements. Some of these might include the following:

1. a prohibition on issuing any mechanical license at a rate lower than 75 percent of the compulsory mechanical licensing rate in the Copyright Law (the statutory rate);

2. a general requirement that no license may be issued on terms less favorable than those reflecting *standard* or *common practice* in the music industry (as a practical matter, it would be difficult to really ascertain what is standard or common, but this type of provision would at least discourage "free" licenses);

3. a requirement that all payments under the license be made *from the source* of the payment to each writer individually (for example, if one writer issues a mechanical license to CBS Records, the license would have to specify that CBS pay each writer's individual share of mechanical royalties directly to that writer);

4. a requirement that, if any payments are inadvertently received by one writer, the individual shares must be paid to each of the other writers within ten days after receipt;

5. a requirement that a copy of any license or other agreement be sent to each songwriter within ten days after being signed; and

6. a requirement that printed or visual credit for each songwriter be given wherever credit for any of the songwriters appears.

The above situation could be expressed in a collaboration agreement, but often a *co-administration agreement* is used. This simply means that more than one songwriter or company has the *administration rights* (the rights to issue licenses and collect income) to some share of the song. A co-administration agreement specifies percentages and limitations such as those described above, sometimes prohibiting either company from exercising rights to anything other than its own share of the musical composition. I'll be discussing these agreements again later.

If you're a songwriter with a much stronger interest in a jointly created song than the other writers, either because the song has been written solely for your musical group or because you are the only writer actively involved in the promotion and "deal-making" for the song, *none* of the alternatives above will probably be appropriate. In your situation, you may wish to have your co-writers enter into an administration or *co-publishing agreement* giving you the *only* right to issue licenses and collect money concerning the song. You would still be required to pay your co-writers their stated income participation shares at certain specific times (for example, at the end of every

> You might agree that after one year, if no music publishing agreement acceptable to all of the writers is offered for the song, and if no other approved use of the song has occurred by that time, the writers may take back their individual creative contributions to the song.

six months or every calendar quarter), but you would not need approval for your decisions concerning the song.

A *co-publishing agreement* refers to a split of music publishing ownership and music publishing income between two songwriters or companies. As I've discussed in this chapter, the "natural" legal state of collaboration is a co-publishing situation, because even without an agreement, two or more songwriters jointly own the song they've written and have equal co-administration rights. A formal co-publishing agreement or administration agreement, however, can specify that a copyright is technically owned by two or more writers or companies, but that only *one* writer or company has the right to issue licenses and collect money for the song.

If your situation is the one described earlier in this section, where your collaborator is either generally not interested in the business and legal aspects of songwriting, or is usually not physically available for approval over any kind of agreement, or lacks any real understanding of the business, you should have an additional written document attached to any administration or co-publishing agreement. It should be a specific *power of attorney* (in most states, this must be notarized) permitting you to act for that songwriter with respect to any matter concerning their share of the copyright. You should probably even have the right to assign their entire ownership share of the song to a music publisher, producer, or artist if you decide it's necessary (to be fair, you should guarantee to your co-writer in writing that any assignment of music publishing shares to other people or companies will be taken equally from your ownership share and theirs).

▬▬

Collaboration is often a friendly, casual process. That doesn't mean it has to be an ignorant process as well. Protect yourself by understanding your rights as a co-writer and requiring appropriate agreements when necessary.

CHAPTER 4

BUSINESS BY MAIL:
CAUTION IS THE WATCHWORD

So you've finally written a song and all your relatives and friends think it's great! You're not so sure your place in musical history is guaranteed just yet, but after reading the section on copyright in this book, you've decided to register the song with the Copyright Office in Washington, D.C., to give it the best possible protection. Now what do you do?

For the majority of you who live in areas outside the music industry centers of Los Angeles, New York City, and Nashville, you may not know how to find someone to improve the song, make a good demo, or promote your song. Unfortunately, there are many disreputable companies that realize this and offer services that seem to make the whole process incredibly simple. If you don't understand the way the music business works, this can be the beginning of an expensive, painful lesson in the art of deception.

In this chapter, I'll be discussing business by mail with *songsharks*. These companies and individuals prey upon uninformed songwriters, most frequently those living in cities and states far from the mainstream of music industry activity. The mail advertisements and promotions from these shady operators take many forms but always give false hope that they are your quickest and easiest road to success, fame, and fortune.

You shouldn't be surprised if these promotions are sent to your home within six to nine months after you've registered a song with the Copyright Office. Many of these companies apparently search the copyright records to find new copyright registrations and the names of songwriters. For most of you who are approached in this manner, it seems to be the only way these companies could have found you.

Songsharks appear to stay within the letter of the law because technically they do the things they promise. The fraud, however, is that their promotions make it seem that their services are of significant value to you. On the contrary, the services of these companies are of extremely poor quality and are virtually always worthless. The most common schemes fall within the categories below.

Lyric or Composer Services

How many times have you told yourself that you could write a hit song if only you had better lyrics to add to your incredible music, or if only you had more effective music to back up those wonderfully sensitive lyrics you wrote two months ago? Songsharks are aware of your secret desire for collaborators! (In fact, as you'll learn in this chapter, they seem to be totally aware of all your needs. That's why they run very profitable businesses!)

"Send us your lyrics! Our successful composers will make your words come alive!" "We want your music! Our hit lyricists will match the perfect words!" There are, of course, always charges for these services. No matter how small the charges may seem to you, legitimate composers and lyricists do *not* charge their collaborators to create songs, and you should not pay even one dollar for these types of services. In my experience, the quality of the "added" lyrics or music that songwriters "buy" from these companies runs the range from miserable to horrible to a very bad joke.

Songwriter Organizations

What if you don't know any songwriters in your area to write with? There are probably many more available, willing, and able songwriters near you than you think. Contact a local or regional songwriter organization for this information. There's an extensive list of such organizations in the annual *Songwriter's Market*, published by Writer's Digest Books.

Among the most prominent songwriter organizations operating nationally, the National Academy of Songwriters (NAS) maintains a list of songwriters seeking collaborators, as well as the names of other songwriter organizations throughout the country. NAS is located at 6381 Hollywood Boulevard, Suite 780, Hollywood, California 90028, (800) 826-7287 or, in California, (800) 334-1446. In Nashville, contact the Nashville Songwriters Association International, 803 Eighteenth Avenue South, Nashville, Tennessee 37203, (615) 321-5004. Another helpful songwriter organization is the Los Angeles Songwriters Showcase, Box 93759, Hollywood, California 90093, (213) 654-1666. You may also be able to locate collaborators through the Songwriters Guild of America, with offices in Los Angeles at 6430 Sunset Boulevard, Suite 317, Los Angeles, California 90028, (213) 462-1108; in New York City at 276 Fifth Avenue, Suite 306, New York, New York 10001, (212) 686-6820; and in Nashville at 50 Music Square West, #702, Nashville, Tennessee 37203, (615) 329-1782. These organizations can also give you a wealth of information about songwriting technique, promoting your songs, upcoming music industry activities of interest, and the music business in general. You should not hesitate to check with them if you receive a suspicious promotion through the mail. They are major resources for songwriters, and I strongly recommend becoming a member of one or more of them.

An additional organization in Los Angeles can assist you in your search for a collaborator, although it is not primarily a songwriter organization. It's the Musician's Contact Service, 7315 Sunset Boulevard, Hollywood, California 90046, (213) 851-2333. They charge an annual fee for you to be listed as a songwriter seeking collaborators.

Demo Services

You're thrilled with both your lyrics and music, but you just don't own the right home equipment to record a decent demo. To make matters seem even more hopeless, you live in a town where there are no good, reasonably priced recording studios that can produce a good song demo for you. Once again, the songsharks are ready to come to your rescue!

In all fairness, this is the one area of this chapter where there are honest businesses that will charge a reasonable fee through the mail for services of reasonable quality. All of these companies, both good and bad, will make the same promise to produce a "professional quality" recording of your song at a relatively low cost, so how can you tell the difference?

First, be initially suspicious of a demo service that sends you an unsolicited advertisement through the mail. I know that sounds like unreasonable advice, because all kinds of honest local businesses, from your nearest carwash to the corner pizza parlor, send direct mail solicitations all the time. That's why this is certainly not a hard and fast rule, because if you belong to a songwriter organization or have entered a song contest, it's possible that a reputable demo service has rented a mailing list that includes your name and address. Generally, however, high-quality demo services don't have the money to pay for mailing advertisements to large numbers of songwriters, so an approach like that should make you at least somewhat cautious.

Second, avoid demo services that also promise to promote your song to publishers and record companies, because legitimate demo services are almost never in the business of promotion. Publishers and song pluggers (both discussed in later chapters) are the most frequent representatives of songs and songwriters. The most effective of these people haven't even the slightest amount of time to run a demo service for unknown songwriters, because they're far too busy promoting songs by making phone calls and having meetings with recording artists, record producers, and songwriters.

Third, don't deal with any demo service that won't allow you to speak to an actual person over the phone. Many of the worst of these companies only do business through the mail. A legitimate demo service should be able to return your phone call within a reasonable period of time after you call them. The songwriter organizations mentioned above are good sources of referrals to reputable demo services in Los Angeles, Nashville, and New York City. Dealing with honest companies by mail and over the phone should be relatively simple.

Before you send money to *any* kind of demo company through the mail, whether you think they're honest or dishonest, ask for a sample of their work that includes the lead singer they will use for your song. The best way to know if you're likely to be satisfied is to request a copy of a previous demo they've recorded that's in the same general style you want for your song. Also ask them to specify, in writing, what instruments will be used. If you want a particular arrangement or *voicing* (for example, a male vocalist with female background singers, or an alto sax solo), negotiate these things when you talk about a price. Send no money until a demo company has given you a written description of the key elements of your demo, and you are satisfied that you've been given a reasonable assurance of the kind of style and sound you're paying for.

Don't be too impressed by promises of a twenty-four-track demo or a description of the impressive array of state-of-the-art, high-tech equipment that the studio will be using. I've heard a lot of four-track home demos that presented a song more effectively than some careless, badly produced, twenty-four-track tragedies. I've also heard digi-

Before you send money to *any* kind of demo company through the mail, whether you think they're honest or dishonest, ask for a sample of their work that includes the lead singer they will use for your song.

tally recorded demos using Synclaviers and other astronomically expensive equipment that were totally ineffective in presenting a particular song. *The talent and effort of the demo producer make the difference, not the studio and equipment.*

Song Publishers

You're really starting to feel good about your songwriting now. You have a great song and a great demo. How do you promote your song to record companies, recording artists, record producers, the personal managers of recording artists, and motion picture and television production companies? If you don't know how to approach these individuals and companies, or if you haven't got the time and patience, a music publisher is the most common representative of songs and songwriters (see the complete discussion of this in chapter six).

All music publishers will promise to promote your song to the people and companies mentioned above. Even among the best publishers, however, it's impossible to predict who will be able to get your song "cut" or "covered" for records, motion pictures, or television programs. So how do you tell the difference between legitimate publishers and songsharks?

The primary rule in singling out shady operators and phony publishers from legitimate music publishers is whether they charge any kind of cash fee in advance for their services. *Never* (no exceptions) pay a music publisher a preliminary fee for promoting your song or making a demonstration recording, no matter how small an amount is requested.

BMI (Broadcast Music, Inc.) and ASCAP (American Society of Composers, Authors and Publishers), the two major performing rights societies that collect money for the public performance of musical compositions and pay songwriters and publishers who are members, will not allow any music publisher member to charge a songwriter advance fees for publishing services. The performing rights payments collected by ASCAP and BMI are the largest source of income for most hit songs, so does it make sense that a legitimate publisher would disqualify itself from receiving this money? Reputable music publishers make their money from payments by users of the songs, not from the songwriters.

Another clear warning that you are dealing with a songshark publisher is a "blind" solicitation sent to you through the mail. Competent music publishers do not operate this way, because they have neither the need nor the time to conduct a general mail campaign to songwriters. In fact, most of them are usually involved with far more tapes, songs, and songwriters than they have time to handle, so you have to be the one to approach them!

That doesn't mean that publishers never advertise. On the contrary, in *Songwriter's Market*, for example, many smaller, often newer, publishers list their names and mailing addresses for your demo tapes. The editor of that annual directory attempts to screen those listings to make sure they do not charge fees to songwriters. That does not mean, of course, that the names listed in *Songwriter's Market* are necessarily the most successful, established, major publishers in the music industry, or that the agreement they send you is absolutely fair and can be signed without review by an attorney. It does mean that those companies are hungrier for material from new writers than many other music publishers, and that they are easier to reach (and

The primary rule in singling out shady operators and phony publishers from legitimate music publishers is whether they charge any kind of cash fee in advance for their services. *Never* pay a music publisher a preliminary fee for promoting your song or making a demonstration recording.

impress) than many major publishers. Most importantly, though, you can usually be certain that you will not be dealing with a songshark and paying a cash fee.

For other names of legitimate music publishers that may be receptive to your song demos, contact the songwriter organizations listed in this chapter. Also, read music industry trade publications (especially *Billboard* magazine) for listings of hit songs and the names of the music publishing companies that publish them. This information is also usually contained on the records and tapes themselves, either on the outside jacket or on the printed material inside. The majority of these companies are in New York City, Los Angeles, or Nashville, so it's not difficult to find their mailing addresses. You can also contact the offices of BMI or ASCAP to find out the address of a particular publisher member. Don't call them for a general list, because they have far too many publisher members to send you one. In general, call a publisher before sending a tape, because many do not accept unsolicited tapes in the mail. There are excellent, extensive discussions about promoting your songs to music publishers (as well as to others in the entertainment industry) in *The Craft and Business of Songwriting*, written by John Braheny, and *How to Pitch and Promote Your Songs*, by Fred Koller, both published by Writer's Digest Books.

Lyric Publishers

You've finally written the kind of emotional, poetic lyrics you always knew you could write. Your mother cries every time she reads them, and you don't really care if they're ever put to music. If only someone would publish your words in a book so that other people could read and enjoy them, perhaps you would be discovered as a great poet or lyricist. Maybe if you had something in print to impress music publishers and record companies, you would be taken more seriously as a songwriter. Well, our old friends the songsharks are once again more than willing to help you!

Lyric book songsharks use a basic strategy of appealing to your ego. Who doesn't like to see their name in print and have something to show their family and friends? You may see no harm at all in paying a songshark a fee to receive a book of poems or lyrics that includes your work. Don't think for one moment, however, that this printed edition will advance your career as a songwriter or poet in any way.

No matter what promises a lyric book publisher makes as to where the book will be sent or promoted, no one in the music industry pays the least bit of attention to these types of publications. There is absolutely no point in sending a copy of a book like that to a record company, music publisher, or anyone else for promotional purposes. In fact, including a copy with a demo tape would probably hurt your presentation more than it helps, verifying that you are only an amateur at what you do. If you're going to pay to have your work "published" like that, keep the book on your bookshelf!

> You may see no harm at all in paying a songshark a fee to receive a book of poems or lyrics that includes your work. Don't think for one moment, however, that this printed edition will advance your career as a songwriter or poet in any way.

Record Companies

You've got a great song and a great tape, but you haven't been able to get a contract you like from legitimate publishers. You've learned to reject the offers from songshark music publishers, and you've decided to publish and promote your songs yourself. After contacting a number of recording artists and producers, you can't seem to develop any interest, but you still believe you've got a hit on your hands. You wish there were just some way to have a record company record your song and get it to radio stations, because you know the public would love it. Once again, the songsharks have unfortunately read your mind.

As with the other activities discussed above, ignore direct mail solicitations claiming to be interested in hearing your song for potential records. Otherwise, the response you receive will be: "Congratulations! The tape you've submitted has been selected for a test pressing! It will be included on a promotional record sent to hundreds of radio stations across the country!" The payment terms to cover your "pressing" always sound quite reasonable. "Pay just $395 in equal monthly installments! No interest will be charged!" These companies sound like they're run by a wonderful bunch of people.

As I mentioned in the beginning of this chapter, most of these characters avoid criminal prosecution by actually doing what they say they'll do. Record company songsharks really *will* record your song. I've heard some of these pitiful products over the years. Usually, only three or four instruments are used, and the track sounds like it was recorded on the first performance with no rehearsal and an absolute minimum of professional sound mixing. I've never heard a songshark production that sounds even remotely effective enough to attract the attention of anyone in the public or the music industry.

These record companies will also send some kind of amateurish promotional package to radio stations, where they are virtually always thrown immediately in the trash. Program directors of radio stations don't have the time or desire to search for hits this way, so don't think that your song has even the remotest chance of becoming popular or earning you any money through this process. This is true whether it's the largest station in your area or the smallest. Even if an occasional radio station staff member listened out of curiosity, the technical and artistic quality of these test pressings doesn't come close to that of the records released and distributed by legitimate record companies. It's hard to imagine any program director or disc jockey risking a loss of audience and ratings by playing such garbage.

> You have a far better chance of having your own carefully produced song played by a small, local station if you try to meet with the program director yourself.

You have a far better chance of having your own carefully produced song played by a small, local station if you try to meet with the program director yourself. Bear in mind, though, that this is also a long shot. Most radio stations have a very tight programming format and have no room on their playlists for local, independently produced records unless the recording artist is very popular in that region.

To show you how carefully planned the songshark strategies described in this chapter are, it's even common for two or more of these types of deceptive services to be related. For example, a lyrical or composing service will offer to produce your demo—for an extra charge, of course—in addition to providing the service you paid for initially.

In one case I investigated a few years ago, a songwriter made cash payments to: (1) a demo service that added lyrics to his music and promised to send the finished tape to publishers; (2) a music publisher that received the tape from the demo service, charging a fee to promote it to record companies; and (3) a record company that received the tape from the publisher, accepting it for a "test pressing" at the songwriter's expense. All of these companies had different names and different Hollywood addresses, so the writer had thought this was all a dream come true—surely his ticket to fame and fortune! A brief search of business ownership records revealed that all three companies were owned by the same corporation. This corporation even published an informational newsletter and various books for songwriters, all at outrageously high prices, that discussed the practices of its secret subsidiaries as normal, advisable ways to achieve success!

Now you've learned enough to keep yourself, your songs, and your money out of the hands of people who are in business to take unfair advantage of your dreams. Here's a brief review of rules for doing business by mail:

1. Unless you're a member of a songwriter organization that may rent its mailing list to advertisers, be immediately suspicious of any direct mail promotion for songwriter services. Be especially wary of any mail you receive that could only have been the result of a search of Copyright Office registration records. (You should be aware that some song contests also compile mailing lists this way. Read the next chapter to determine whether entering a particular contest is in your best interest.)

2. *Never* pay a lyricist or composer to collaborate with you. Rely upon songwriter organizations and associations if you don't have contact with enough other songwriters where you live.

3. Carefully screen demo service companies. If you live in an area without adequate demo facilities, doing business by mail with them may be your only alternative. Protect yourself by hearing samples of their work and by committing them to a specific lead voice and a particular musical arrangement. Be sure you have a reasonable expectation of quality for your money.

4. *Never* pay a publisher to accept your song. There are *no* exceptions to this rule.

5. Pay a company to publish your lyrics only if you like the idea of having a printed booklet with your name to show your family and friends.

6. *Never* pay a record company to record your song, no matter how attractive they make their distribution and promotion sound.

7. In general, be suspicious of *any* promotion that makes success in the music industry sound easy!

8. Understand the process by which songs are promoted and selected for recording, and you will be able to develop an effective telephone and mail strategy for sending demonstration recordings of your song to recording artists, producers, publishers, managers, and record companies. (Read the two books recommended earlier in this chapter!) A professional approach is the best approach, and there is nothing professional about the way songsharks record and promote your songs.

9. Make it your business to learn the music business!

CHAPTER 5

SONG CONTESTS:
WHEN IS A PRIZE NOT A PRIZE?

You've probably heard the expression "everybody loves a winner." An equally true expression would be "everybody wants to be a winner," because winning in our society has always meant success of some kind. Whether it relates to a job, a romance, a sports event, or a contest, we all want to feel like we're winners in some aspect of our lives.

If we can't be winners through some normal accomplishment or activity, there are a number of other ways that have become available. Over the past ten years or so, it seems the basic human need to "be a winner" has inspired a multitude of lotteries, contests, and prize promotions offered by state governments, corporations, and organizations of every description and there appears to be an endless public demand for these events.

Music Industry Contests

The music industry is no exception. From the national exposure of television competitions like *Star Search*, to national songwriting and performing contests conducted through the mail, to even the most basic local contest sponsored by a retail store looking for an advertising theme song, the promotions go on and on, each fueled by the dreams of aspiring songwriters and performers. This chapter will discuss the ways that many of these kinds of competitions take unfair advantage of those of you who see these events as your big chance to be winners in the music industry.

The contests and competitions in the music industry differ in one important respect from the general "random chance" prize promotions commonly directed to the general public: Luck is not a factor, as the contestants are presumably judged on talent. Additionally, the entrants hope to receive some form of publicity or recognition that will advance their careers. These overriding motivations, as well as whatever monetary prizes may be involved, unfortunately blind many songwriters and performers to the "fine print" of these contests.

To begin with, you should not have any illusions or unrealistic expectations about the relationship of these contests to the legitimate, mainstream commercial music industry. Despite the fact that some competitions use major recording stars, music publishers, songwriters, record producers, or record company executives as judges, contest winners won't necessarily be "discovered" and become rich and famous. In fact, that is rarely the case, even for the most well-known of these contests. As this is written, even most of the winners of *Star Search* competitions who were later signed by record labels have realized only limited commercial success when confronted by the *real* judges in the music industry—radio stations and the general public.

Do not conclude from this chapter that there are no honest, reputable, or worthwhile contests. There certainly are. For many songwriters and recording artists, winning any kind of contest might provide new confidence to aggressively pursue a career that had been stalled. Additionally, whether or not you win a particular contest, it's possible you'll make valuable contacts with music industry professionals who were involved in the judging process, especially if there is any type of social event scheduled for the judges that you're allowed to attend. At the very least (again assuming some form of social event), you'll probably meet other talented songwriters who may collaborate with you in the future.

For whatever psychological, financial, or "networking" benefits you may be seeking, the most prestigious and publicized contests should probably be considered. You should always be cautious, however, and never let your visions of stardom, big prizes, and major connections interfere with your judgment and common sense.

Regardless of the sponsor, the grand prize, the type of contest, how easy it is to enter, or how easy it looks to win, you should always read every printed rule and condition that will apply to your entry.

Contest Rules

Regardless of the sponsor, the grand prize, the type of contest, how easy it is to enter, or how easy it looks to win, you should always read every printed rule and condition that will apply to your entry. These terms and provisions will usually appear on the entry form, but sometimes they can only be found in an advertisement for the contest or some other promotional material. *Read and save everything.* In many contests, you'll be sent a letter *after* you've entered describing special conditions that apply to some final round of competition for which you've been selected. By that time, the people running the contest probably know that you'll be too excited to care about any further rules.

Entry Forms Are Like Contracts

It's critical to understand that, when you enter a contest, you also might be entering into an enforceable agreement on very unfavorable terms. Believe it or not, you don't have to be given an obvious, formal contract to be legally bound by an agreement! Just by sending in the entry form, you've probably consented to all of the conditions printed in the advertisements and other promotional materials for the contest.

In one song contest promotion a few years ago, the entry form contained language that assigned the copyright for each song entered to the sponsor merely upon submission of the entry! Win or lose, the entered songs became the property of the contest company. It's hard to believe, but the thousands of people who entered that contest actually paid a company entry fees just to take their music publishing rights! How is that any different from the songshark publisher discussed in the last chapter who takes money to publish your song? When you find out the answer, please let me know.

I'm not suggesting that you should never give away your music publishing rights in a contest situation. If you win a cash prize that's large enough, it *might* be reasonable to transfer your music publishing rights to the contest sponsor. The point is that it's *never* reasonable to give up any substantial rights whatsoever to a song that doesn't win any prize at all.

Also, after you read chapter six on music publishing agreements, you should understand that even when you assign your music publishing rights to someone, you should *never* give away your rights to the songwriter's share of income from a song. This would be a total *buyout* of your songwriting *and* music publishing rights and is absolutely inappropriate for *any* type of contest, regardless of the prize to be awarded.

Even when a sponsor only requires that you grant certain rights if your song wins their contest, you must be careful to compare the potential value of what you are giving up and the value of the promised prize. For example, although a cash prize of $2,500 might seem attractive enough to give away your music publishing rights, what if the contest sponsor has only a very limited use in mind for your song? Will the $2,500 be the last income you'll ever receive from that song? Remember, owners of a copyright in a song have virtually complete control over how the song is used, and you will not even be able to use your own song again without their permission.

What's the Prize?

Sometimes a contest sponsor does not require a transfer of ownership or control of music publishing rights in exchange for a prize, but the prize still might not be valuable enough to accept the conditions imposed. An example would be a sponsor holding a contest primarily to find a song for its own commercial promotions.

In one song contest I reviewed, the prize was a free trip to Nashville to appear on a national television show with a country music star. After various songs had been picked to be in the final round of competition, the sponsoring company sent an agreement to the songwriters that required the right to exploit their songs without limit for any form of promotional use. The sponsor was a major manufacturer of consumer products.

The first problem with this requirement was that the contest sponsor would be able to use even the *losing* songs in the final round for promotional use forever and at no charge. Under other circumstances, if any of these songs became a major hit, an advertiser would have to pay a few hundred thousand dollars or more to use it in a national ad campaign. Even for the winning song, this smart sponsor was obtaining a perpetual right to use the song for promotional purposes in exchange for the price of two round-trip airline tickets to Nashville!

In situations like the one described above, rules given to contest entrants after

> It's *never* reasonable to give up any substantial rights whatsoever to a song that doesn't win any prize at all.

they've sent in their entry fee are usually unenforceable. As mentioned earlier, your written entry form, payment of an entry fee, and the initial printed rules of entry usually constitute a valid legal agreement. One of two parties to an agreement cannot, without the consent of the other party, change the terms of the agreement later whenever they desire. Of course, the contest sponsor may not agree with this basic legal principle when you decide to make this legal claim after you've won. If you don't like these "later" rules that were not made available when you entered the contest, the safest policy is to demand that your entry fee be refunded immediately.

Publishing Agreements as Prizes

What about competitions offering some kind of agreement as the prize? Suppose, for example, that you've entered a contest where one of the prizes is a music publishing agreement. You've always wanted to have your song published, right? The promise of a publishing contract with "MAJOR, SUPER, FANTASTIC MUSIC of Los Angeles, California," sounds impressive, doesn't it? If entry fees are required for the contest (which will certainly be the case), why are you paying money just for the chance to have someone publish your song? In the case of many music publishers, you can probably submit the song directly to them without entering the contest. If your song is good enough to win, it's good enough to merit a music publishing agreement without a contest competition. Also, you should be aware that being offered a music publishing agreement is not even the remotest guarantee that your song will be recorded and exploited in a way that will make any money for you.

Even when you think an agreement offered as a prize is worth competing for, unless you see the agreement in advance, you may be totally wasting your entry money. Virtually always in contests of this type, you will not be able to see the provisions of the prize agreement until you win. What will the terms of the agreement be? If a publishing agreement is offered as a prize, will the publisher give the rights to your song back to you if there is no commercial recording and use within a limited time period? Will the royalty and accounting provisions be standard? These questions should be answered before you risk any of your hard-earned cash to be "awarded" an agreement with unknown terms.

One of two parties to an agreement cannot, without the consent of the other party, change the terms of the agreement later whenever they desire.

Recording Contracts as Prizes

What if you're also a performer who's looking for a record deal for yourself or your group? There are some contests that offer major recording contracts as prizes. You'd probably sell your grandmother to win a recording contract, right? You should be aware that the prize contract proposal might be unreasonable, and that the company offering the agreement might be unwilling to negotiate and revise the key terms and provisions. There can be other major complications you never dreamed of while you were planning what to do with the first million dollars you figured you'd make from the prize record deal.

I represented the winner in one competition for a recording contract who ended up with nothing but heartbreak and frustration, and he wishes now he had never entered the contest. The first hint of future trouble appeared after the selection of the performers for the final round of judging (which always seems to be the ideal time for contest sponsors to spring their little legal surprises on the finalists). At that point, the record company offering the prize agreement insisted that a *right of first negotiation/first refusal* be signed by the finalists. They all agreed.

Under the terms of the document, which all finalists had to sign in order to remain eligible for the final round of judging, the winner of the contest would have professional demonstration recordings produced by the record label. Sounds pretty attractive so far, right? The winner would then be required to negotiate only with *that* record label for a period of two to four months after the completion of the demonstration recordings. Well, the record company paid for the recordings, so it sounds pretty fair to negotiate with them first, don't you think?

Contractual provisions in the music industry are almost never as simple and fair as they seem. The first problem was that there was no time limit for recording the demos, so the artist could have been made to wait indefinitely until the demos were finished. If any other record label was interested in the artist in the meantime, the artist had no right to even talk to that label, because the winner had no option to either refuse the demonstration recordings or refuse to negotiate. The second major problem was that, once the demonstration recordings were completed, even if the negotiations for the recording contract failed, the winner still had a legal obligation to the record company. If the winner was offered another agreement by another record label at *any time within two years*, the original record label (the contest sponsor) had the absolute right to sign the performer to its own contract (the same agreement rejected by the artist already) for 90 percent of the financial value (advances and royalties) of the offer from the second record label—with no further negotiation! What a deal! What a prize!

As you might have expected from my sarcastic description, the ending to this story was not happy in the least. Although I suppose I shouldn't criticize this performer too harshly for taking a calculated gamble on a chance for national publicity and exposure through a major record deal, the situation turned out to be more of a continuing nightmare than a prize. By the end of the relationship with the record label, more than an entire year of the performer's career efforts had been wasted with endless arguments and fruitless negotiations. No demonstration recordings were ever made. No record deal was ever signed. No records were ever released. No star was born. Most significantly, in the end nobody really had "won" anything.

Now you're too scared and suspicious to ever enter another contest, right? Aren't there any kinds of conditions that are reasonable for a contest sponsor to require for the songs or performances of contest winners? Of course there are.

1. Always begin by making sure you completely understand the description of the prize and its real value to you. You'll then be in a better position to evaluate whether all of the rules and requirements that apply to you either before or after you've won a particular competition are reasonable.

2. Generally, it's fair to give the contest sponsor the right to use a winning song or performance (or even a song or performance merely in the final round of competition) in connection with any promotion of the contest, any awards ceremony, or any television program or motion picture concerning the contest or awards ceremony. Remember that there's a big difference between this right and giving contest sponsors the unlimited right to use a song to promote a commercial product or promote their business generally. Always be extremely

careful before you agree to give away any kinds of rights that appear to be unrestricted.

3. If a contest sponsor intends to sell records or tapes containing winning songs to the public, mechanical royalties (which I'll discuss later) should be paid to the songwriters. If a performance by you or your group will also be contained on the records, you should receive payments in the normal range of recording artist royalties. If you've produced the recording released for sale to the public, you should also receive producer's royalties.

4. Should you avoid all music industry competitions? Of course not. Many are sponsored and run by reputable organizations and companies that offer only legitimate prizes with no unreasonable conditions attached to either the winners or the entrants in general.

5. How can you protect yourself? Read every advertisement, every piece of promotional material, and every other scrap of paper involving the contest you are entering. When you discover any language concerning any type of right or obligation you owe to the sponsor or anyone else connected with the competition, contact an attorney to explain the legal effect of the requirements. Otherwise, you might be entering into an enforceable agreement without knowing it.

6. If a contest sponsor tries to impose any unacceptable conditions *after* you've entered a contest, whether as part of a final round of competition or otherwise, the conditions are probably legally unenforceable. It's safest, however, to immediately demand that your entry fee be refunded.

Some music competitions can be immensely worthwhile and rewarding. Now you can prevent your prize from being a surprise.

CHAPTER 6

SINGLE-SONG TRANSFERS OF MUSIC PUBLISHING RIGHTS

Suppose you've written a great song and have sent it to many music publishers, producers, personal managers, and recording artists. Eventually, someone contacts you and absolutely loves your song. They also tell you they want the *publishing* or the *music publishing rights*. What do they mean?

They are referring to all of the rights of copyright discussed in chapter one: the rights to own and control all uses of your song and collect the money from those uses (they should still pay you a portion of the money collected, though, as discussed later in this chapter). This is different from when someone only wants to use your song for a record, motion picture, television program, or in some other way *without* requiring your music publishing rights. In chapter nine, I'll explain *self-publishing*, where you issue *direct licenses* (permissions) to users of your song without giving them ownership or control. This chapter will describe the kinds of agreements that deal with transferring total or partial ownership or control of your music publishing rights.

Who Will Want Your Music Publishing Rights?

There are many different people and companies that might want these rights. These include record producers, recording artists, personal managers, record companies, recording studios, investors, motion picture production companies, television production companies, and, of course, music publishing companies that *only* engage in music publishing activities. The term *music publisher* might confuse you, because almost anyone in the music industry who wants your publishing rights will handle administration (management) of those rights under their own music publishing company (or at least one affiliated with them). So all of the individuals and companies listed above might technically be music publishers!

Virtually all music publishers will want to have exclusive rights to your song. Once you sign this type of agreement for a particular song, you will not be able to give any rights of ownership or control to anyone else unless the music publisher gives your rights back to you (*reassigns*) at some later date. You will also be unable to give permission for anyone else to use your song or to prevent your publisher from giving permission for a particular use of your song (maybe you don't like dog food commercials), because you no longer own or control your own work!

There was a classic case in the 1980s illustrating how strictly this principle of exclusive ownership is applied. Fantasy Records, which owns the copyrights for most of the songs John Fogarty wrote for Creedence Clearwater Revival in the late 1960s and early 1970s, filed a legal action claiming he infringed the copyright *in his own song*, "Run Through the Jungle," when he wrote the song "Old Man Down the Road" for his 1985 album *Centerfield*. Attempting to avoid a trial, Fogarty's attorneys argued that a music publisher could not legally sue a songwriter for infringing his own work, because a songwriter is a "beneficial" owner of the copyright, and co-owners of copyrights cannot sue each other for copyright infringement. The court rejected that argument and held that a songwriter who assigns his exclusive music publishing rights retains an *economic* interest in his song *but does not have an independent right to use or license the use of the work*. A music publisher therefore *can* sue a songwriter for infringing a song created by the songwriter and transferred to the publisher! Fortunately for Fogarty, the court eventually decided that he did not infringe "Run Through the Jungle" when he wrote "Old Man Down the Road."

You can see now why assigning exclusive music publishing rights for one or more of your songs is an act of major legal significance, especially if you feel that a particular song is by far your best. You should therefore be very careful in determining who should have these rights for any substantial period of time. How do you decide?

Professional Music Publishers

The most common offers of music publishing agreements you'll receive will come from full-time music publishers. As I'll discuss in the next section, some of these publishers might want to acquire the rights to your song because it's being used by one of their affiliated record, motion picture, or television companies. In this section, however, I'm referring to the situation where a publisher acquires your song and *then* promotes it to record producers, recording artists, motion picture producers, and other "users" of music. The best of them will also help develop your career by helping you to improve your songwriting, introducing you to new collaborators, and paying for demonstration recordings of your songs.

The track record or status of a particular publisher may or may not be helpful in choosing among companies. The largest publishers own vast catalogs of active hit songs, but the majority of uses for these songs may have come from inquiries and requests that were not the result of any active promotion by the publisher's current employees. Also, your song may not receive the attention it deserves among the hundreds of songs being created by the established *staff writers* for such a company (staff writers are discussed in the next chapter). On the other hand, some of the largest companies are closely affiliated with major record, motion picture, and television

Virtually all music publishers will want to have exclusive rights to your song. Once you sign this type of agreement for a particular song, you will not be able to give any rights of ownership or control to anyone else unless the music publisher gives your rights back to you (*reassigns*) at some later date.

companies, providing a greater likelihood that your song will be used for a major recording.

The newest, smallest publishers may have no hits or other recordings to their credit, but they may be extremely selective in signing songs and in aggressively promoting a small catalog. Then there's the middle ground — major independent publishers without affiliated record, motion picture, or television branches but with a sufficient track record of success to make you confident in their promotional skills.

Which type of publisher is best? If you're still confused, you're not alone. Many songwriters find it difficult to choose between the experience and clout of a large publisher and the individual, personal attention of a smaller company. Even the most established music publishing companies cannot guarantee they will be able to obtain a use for your song that will make money or gain you any degree of notoriety. Nonetheless, it's usually a good idea to ask all publishers, regardless of size, what ideas they have for possible recordings. If they don't appear to have the slightest notion of who might record your song (this is called *casting* the song), you should look for another publisher. A competent publisher should be able to think of at least a few casting ideas.

I usually recommend assigning one or two songs to a few *different* types of publishers (you remember what your grandmother told you about not putting all your eggs in one basket). Regardless of which type of publisher you choose, as long as you get a reasonable *reversion clause* (discussed later), the rights to your song will not be tied up for a long period of time unless it's recorded for a commercial use.

User Publishers

For many of you, the actual *user* of your song will be the first to want the music publishing rights. That is their "condition" for recording your song for a record release, a motion picture soundtrack, or a television program.

There are two basic reasons why motion picture and television producers acquire music publishing rights. First, as I've already discussed, owning the copyright in a musical work means control of that music. The producer can grant or refuse to grant licenses (permissions) to others for use of the music and can continue to use the music in the future for promotional purposes, home video products, sequels, spinoffs, and other productions without needing to ask for permission again and without making any additional payment to the songwriter. Second, if the picture or program (or the music separately) is successful, the producer can generate substantial extra income.

Record producers who require your music publishing rights have the same basic motivations. They want ownership, control, and extra income.

In one sense, transferring music publishing rights to a user of music may be desirable because there is no speculation about what will happen to your song. The contract should specify that it will be used in a certain way in exchange for the transfer of music publishing rights. You should be aware that under some circumstances, however, these types of music publishing transfers can totally destroy the value of a great song.

In the case of motion picture and television producers, for instance, very few have the knowledge or motivation to exploit music profitably when their production has otherwise been an economic disaster. In fact, when their projects are failures, either

> Ask all publishers, regardless of size, what ideas they have for possible recordings. If they don't appear to have the slightest notion of who might record your song, you should look for another publisher. A competent publisher should be able to think of at least a few casting ideas.

because they were never completed or because they were not financially successful when exploited, virtually all television and motion picture producers merely take their tax write-offs and move on the other projects.

Similar problems can occur with record producers who own your copyright. If a recording artist project has not been commercially successful, the producer will most likely lose faith in the songs involved.

Regardless of who uses your music, if you've transferred ownership of potentially valuable songs that were included in a failed project, it's likely that the music in that production will meet a premature death. Like any other music publisher, a user of music who also owns and controls the copyright should either continue attempting to exploit the song or offer to reassign all rights to the songwriters in exchange for return of any fees paid.

I was involved in a matter a few years ago where a motion picture producer paid a songwriter to write a number of separate musical compositions for the producer's picture. The producer also acquired all of the music publishing rights in exchange for the same fee. The picture was released for only a few weeks, in only a few theaters, with virtually no public or critical response, and all further exploitation was abandoned.

The writer later became employed as a staff (exclusive) songwriter by a major music publishing company with a reputation for obtaining many successful recordings for the songs in their catalog. Upon hearing some songs the writer had composed for the picture, a major creative force in the company wanted to obtain the rights to a particular song he felt could become a classic hit. Months of effort in attempting to contact the motion picture producer and offering to repurchase either all or some of the rights to the song met with no success. The songwriter and publisher finally just requested the right to grant licenses for recording the song and the right to collect the income, offering to pay the producer his normal publisher's share of income. The producer was not interested in discussing the matter, and to my knowledge he has never made any attempt to promote or exploit any of the songs in the picture.

That particular music publisher later placed a song on the first Whitney Houston album, which sold over ten million copies and generated far more income for each songwriter and music publisher involved than the motion picture producer ever realized from his failed project. The song the producer stubbornly refused to discuss or promote might have been on that album (where it would have earned him well over six figures for just his music publishing share), or on the album of some other successful artist, or in another motion picture, or in a television program, or used in some other profitable manner—if only the producer had realized that the proper management of music rights for motion pictures and television does not end with the final product that appears on the screen.

How do you protect yourself in these situations? You can almost never obtain a promise of commercial success for your song, but you can at least insist on some basic safeguards guaranteeing that the song will be used in some significant way.

Whatever the nature of the production project, always require that the music be used in the production and that the production be exploited commercially. A motion picture should be released for exhibition to the public. A television program should be broadcast to the public over free, cable, or pay television. A home video product or record should be manufactured and distributed for sale to the public. Whatever

A user of music who also owns and controls the copyright should either continue attempting to exploit the song or offer to reassign all rights to the songwriters in exchange for return of any fees paid.

the use required, a certain date for that use should also be specified. For most uses, you should accept a date no later than one to two years after the date of the contract. For a motion picture, some songwriters also insist that a soundtrack album be released for sale to the public within three to six months after the first public exhibition of the picture.

If the specific use described in the contract does not occur within the time limit stated, all rights to your song should revert to you automatically. You should be prepared, however, to return any money paid to you for the song at the time of reversion.

For the reasons I've just described, full-time music publishers do not generally like to see transfers of music publishing rights to companies that are not *full-service* music publishers. They believe these companies will not continue to promote and exploit a song after an initial recording, and if the particular use is unsuccessful (like the failed movie I mentioned or an album that sells only a few copies), the song will be "dead" for all practical purposes. They also feel these types of publishers will not become involved in the improvement and development of a songwriter's career.

Assuming you don't want to be your own publisher, you should only assign your music publishing rights for a particular song to a person or company that will either: (a) develop and promote the song; (b) develop and promote your career as a song-writer or recording artist; or (c) use the song in a way likely to generate income or give you notoriety. You should generally avoid most other transfers of music publishing rights.

I'm referring to individuals and companies who will hold your music publishing rights merely hoping that they will be worth something someday. These might include people outside the music industry who only invest money in your demos or career (in chapter eleven, I'll discuss more appropriate ways to compensate investors), or recording studios who require music publishing rights in exchange for free studio time.

I cannot emphasize strongly enough the importance of your music publishing rights. If you give these rights away too early to the wrong company for the wrong reason or transfer rights to too many songs to a company that is not successful in promoting or using your works, you might destroy your bargaining power for more important deals later. Also, always remember that the improper exercise of ownership and control of these rights or just a failure to do anything at all with the rights can "kill" a song. Music publishing rights should only be assigned after careful thought and consideration.

So you've read all my warnings and you've spent all of thirty seconds deciding that you want to deal with SUPERHITS MUSIC from Los Angeles, California, because you noticed that they control the music publishing rights to every song on the most recent hit album by Sally Superstar. They send you a contract. Now what do you do?

Most people would tell you to call a music industry attorney, and that's certainly the safest course of action. You can save a lot of money on legal fees, though, by understanding at least the basic terms of music publishing agreements. You should then be able to determine for yourself whether a particular agreement is generally acceptable *before* you hire an attorney.

You can save a lot of money on legal fees by understanding at least the basic terms of music publishing agreements. You should then be able to determine for yourself whether a particular agreement is generally acceptable *before* you hire an attorney.

Basic Provisions of Single-Song Agreements

The term *single-song* isn't really accurate because often a music publisher will want more than one of your songs and will list all of the titles on the same document. The term really applies to any agreement for transfer of your music publishing rights to songs that are specifically named. The heading of the agreement might be something like "Popular Songwriter's Agreement" or "Standard Songwriter's Agreement" (don't believe it—nothing in the music industry is really "standard"). The major areas of negotiation in single-song agreements are the following:

The Legal Rights to Be Transferred

Most frequently, as discussed above, you will be asked to assign all of your rights to a song. There are various other situations, though, where you will split these rights with a music publisher.

If either you or your song has strong negotiating power (for example, when you've already had recordings of either that song or one of your other songs), or if the music publisher has weak negotiating power (maybe it's a new company with no recordings to its credit), a co-publishing agreement might be possible. Under that kind of agreement, the copyright is owned jointly by you and the music publisher, and you are entitled to some percentage of the *net* music publishing income left over after the publisher has computed your songwriter's share (discussed further under "Royalties and Other Payments"). The stronger your power (or the weaker the publisher's), the greater the extra percentage of ownership and income you can obtain for yourself.

In a straight *administration agreement*, which you can usually obtain if a song is already earning (or is likely to earn) significant income (for example, you obtained a recording of the song by Sally Superstar yourself), the publisher may take no ownership at all, but charge 10 to 15 percent of gross music publishing receipts for issuing licenses and collecting money on your behalf. There are also *co-administration agreements*, where both you and the publisher have the right to issue licenses and collect money. In these situations, each of you will have a duty to *account* (report and pay) to the other for any sums received from the song.

Other aspects of co-publishing, administration, and co-administration agreements are discussed later in this chapter.

The Advance

An *advance* is a sum of money paid to you just for signing a music publishing agreement. Advances are usually *recoupable* (recoverable) from the royalties you would otherwise be owed. For example, if a publisher pays you an advance of $500, and if the publisher receives $1,000 in gross music publishing income, and if the agreement is for the standard 50-50 split of income (see the discussion below), the publisher would keep the entire $1,000. The publisher would then have recouped the advance, and thereafter they would pay you fifty cents from every dollar received.

The dollar amount for single-song advances ranges from "Are you kidding? We never pay advances!" to "Name your price." If you're a new songwriter with no prior recordings, and if the music publisher is a small company, it is unlikely that any advance will be offered. If you are dealing with a major music publisher, you might be able to get an advance in the $200 to $500 range, regardless of your history of success. A major music publisher might even go to $1,000 and beyond for the right song. If you walk through a music publisher's door with a song that is the newly released single by Sally Superstar, and if Sally's recent singles and albums have appeared at the top of the charts and sold millions of copies, you might be offered $10,000 to $50,000 or more for just the co-publishing rights to the song!

Be aware that many music publishers offer an advance only if you will not insist on a *reversion clause* (discussed in the next section). In my opinion, this is a poor trade-off, because the reversion clause is critical to the life of your song. A much better position is to insist upon both an advance *and* a reversion clause, agreeing that the rights to the song cannot "revert" to you until you've repaid the advance.

Term of the Agreement

This refers to the length of time the agreement will be in effect. Most publishers want to own and control your rights for the "life of the copyright," which is generally the length of your life plus fifty years! Under U.S. Copyright Law, they can't really have your song that long even if you agreed.

When Congress revised the copyright laws in the 1970s, it was determined that the creator of a work subject to copyright probably wouldn't realize the true value of the work when it was initially transferred to someone else, so a right of *termination of transfer* was provided to give back the rights to the creator after thirty-five to forty years (depending on the circumstances). Unfortunately, for a song that hasn't been exploited, it is doubtful that much value will remain after thirty-five years.

To adequately protect yourself, an essential part of any music publishing agreement is a *reversion clause*. This language should require that a specific use be made of the song within a certain time period, or else all rights to the song *revert* (come back) to you at the end of that time period.

The more specific the language of the reversion clause, the better the protection for you. Some publishers make the language as broad as possible to make it easy to keep the rights to the song. For example, "If the song is not published in saleable form within one year, all rights transferred hereunder shall revert to the songwriter." What is "saleable form"? Can the publisher print one copy and sell it to one local store to keep the song? Other publishers will provide language requiring only a "commercial recording and release" (in my opinion, this is also a bit too general).

As with many terms of a music publishing agreement, the language you can get will depend upon your bargaining power. If you've had four different offers for the song, be tough! You may want to require that the song by commercially recorded and released for sale to the public featuring a recording artist signed to a major label. (You'll need to define "major label," of course). Or you may also agree that an appropriate use is the synchronization (discussed in chapter one) of the song in either the soundtrack of a television program broadcast over a major network during prime time or the soundtrack of a motion picture distributed by a major motion picture company.

How long should the reversion period be? That depends on the use you've required and the wording of the provision, but generally one or two years is considered enough time by many publishers. Some might request three or more years, but in my opinion the vast majority of music publishers will not actively promote a song for that long without results. Regardless of the length of the period requested, you might

An essential part of any music publishing agreement is a *reversion clause*.

agree upon what I call a *split reversion period*. For example, the song must be *recorded* for the specified use within the first nine months, one year, or eighteen months, but the *actual* use (for example, release of the record, exhibition of the motion picture, broadcast of the television program) need not occur until the end of a second period of nine months, one year, or eighteen months.

In addition, try to be sure that the reversion is automatic. Many publishers use language requiring written notice from you. That sounds fair enough, but many of these provisions limit the available notice period to a very narrow span of time (often thirty days). If you forget to mark your calendar properly and miss your deadline, the song will belong to the publisher for thirty-five to forty years. Also, especially in the case of smaller publishers, what happens if a company "disappears" or goes out of business with no forwarding address? Where do you send the notice? Technically, your copyright still belongs to someone else whom you now can't find for purposes of submitting your reversion notice.

Territory

This refers to the geographical scope of your transfer of rights. Virtually always, especially for a song that has not been recorded, a music publisher will insist on at least worldwide rights. Many agreements, optimistically foreseeing a rosy, profitable future for your song in outer space, require rights to the solar system or universe. One agreement I saw, not content with the limitations of the solar system or universe, actually required all "extraterrestrial" rights!

In a situation where your song has already been recorded in the United States, and where you are comfortable with *self-publishing* (discussed in chapter nine) and collecting income in this country, you may be able to negotiate a single-song agreement for either a limited foreign territory or for all countries outside the United States. For example, if your song has been recorded and released by Sally Superstar in the U.S., you may be content to collect your mechanical royalties and small performance royalties here without assistance. You could then find a major worldwide publisher to handle administration for all countries *outside* the U.S., or you could retain a foreign subpublisher to collect income in a single country or major territory (for example, Japan or Western Europe). The same would be true if your song is *only* released in one foreign country or territory; you could limit your music publishing agreement to that area. (Foreign subpublishing agreements are discussed in greater detail in chapter nine.)

Royalties and Other Payments

The "standard" version of a single-song agreement should entitle you to at least 50 percent of most sums the music publisher collects for uses of your song. If you've negotiated some form of co-publishing agreement, you will get an additional percentage, although usually the publisher will give you a separate document covering this percentage (the title of the other agreement will probably be "Participation Agreement" or "Co-Publishing Agreement," discussed below).

One common exception to the *50-percent rule* remains the area of royalties from print rights to uses such as sheet music, dance orchestrations, etc. Among many major music publishers, it has long been a custom to pay a cents-per-copy rate for print uses of songs. These are usually in the range of five to ten cents per copy sold. It's the sole

The "standard" version of a single-song agreement should entitle you to at least 50 percent of most sums the music publisher collects for uses of your song.

area of a songwriter's income that's not close to 50 percent of the publisher's receipts, because as this is written, music publishers receive in the range of fifty to sixty cents per copy sold for these uses.

Royalties for some print music categories (for example, *folios* that contain more than one song) may also be expressed as a percentage of the wholesale price of the product. Most music publishers that use this formula will pay you 10 percent of the wholesale price, although 12 1/2 percent of the wholesale price is usually closer to 50 percent of what the publisher receives for this type of product. If you're dealing with a smaller or newer publisher that probably doesn't have a firm tradition in this area, try to convince them to simplify all of their print music royalties by just paying you 50 percent of their receipts from your songs.

In the area of royalties for small performances, the entire songwriter's share will be paid to you directly by your performing rights society (usually ASCAP or BMI) and the entire publisher's share will be paid directly to the publisher. No music publisher should ever request that you assign to them your right to receive the songwriter's portion of these royalties. In co-publishing situations (discussed below), music publishers will probably want to collect the entire publisher's share and pay you from their receipts.

From all other income sources, including mechanical royalties, synchronization payments, receipts from foreign countries, etc., you should be paid at least 50 percent of the music publisher's receipts. Even this simple equation is a potential trap. If your music publisher hires an outside administrator to manage your song for 15 percent of gross receipts, your publisher will only receive 85 cents for each dollar collected, and you will then be owed only 42 1/2 cents (50 percent of the publisher's receipts). You should make sure that, at least in agreements where you are assigning all of your music publishing rights (that is, a full 50 percent share of music publishing income), the publisher must deduct any outside administration fees from its share of income. One normal exception to this is the fee charged by the Harry Fox Agency (now approximately 4 to 5 percent), a company many publishers use to collect mechanical royalties from record companies.

> Watch out for a publishing company that charges its own administration fee in addition to retaining its normal percentage of music publishing receipts.

Another common exception is the area of foreign royalties, where a foreign subpublisher will deduct a share of foreign receipts prior to sending money to your publisher. Your publisher will then compute the money due you based on the receipts in the United States. If you have strong negotiating power, though, you might be able to require that your foreign royalties by computed *at the source*. This means that you will be owed 50 percent (or whatever other percentage is yours under any co-publishing agreement) based upon the monies collected in the country of sale, *not* the monies received in the U.S. *after* deduction by a foreign subpublisher of its fee.

Also watch out for a publishing company that charges its own administration fee *in addition to retaining its normal percentage of music publishing receipts*. This has the same effect on you as the situation where a 15 percent fee is deducted by an outside administrator before your publisher computes what you are owed, except it's the *publisher* that keeps this extra money! Don't accept excuses and arguments on this issue! The 50 percent share of income that you're already transferring for your song should *always* cover the publisher's administration fees and costs. Be quick to recognize various equations that attempt to hide the fact that you will be receiving less than 50 percent of the publisher's receipts.

There is another paragraph of music publishing agreements that can materially affect what you get paid: the right of the publisher to change your song. Many songwriters have a problem in general with anyone changing their songs without permission, and many publishers will at least agree that they must offer the original songwriters the "first opportunity" to make any changes requested by the publisher. Most publishers, however, reserve the absolute right to change the song. Many songwriters have no problem with this but don't realize that the language of the agreement may permit the publisher to reduce their royalties in order to pay other songwriters for the changes. With the exception of foreign translations or new foreign lyrical versions of your song, without your consent a music publisher should *never* have the right to reduce your royalties for changes made to your song by other songwriters.

Accounting

These provisions are usually simple, but there are certain things to watch for. For example, with only one exception, never let a publisher have the right to retain or hold *reserves* of royalties. A *reserve* provision allows a publisher to keep royalties (that would otherwise be payable to you) for extra periods of time, earning interest on *your* money. The exception would be receipts from a publisher's *direct* sale of print music to distributors, because the distributors will usually be allowed to return these products to the publisher for a refund. Other than that, any money received by a publisher from a licensee (such as a record company or motion picture producer) is nonreturnable, and there is no justification whatsoever for any form of reserves.

Also, most accounting provisions state that you will be considered to have accepted a particular accounting statement unless you have objected within a certain period of time, or that you will be unable to maintain a legal action against the publisher unless it is filed within another specified period of time. These types of provisions are totally effective and enforceable in most states, so make sure the time periods are not too brief. You should have at least eighteen months to two years after you've received an accounting statement to object or file a legal action against a publisher. I've seen agreements that attempt to limit this time period to thirty, sixty, or ninety days!

There should be some provision allowing you to "audit" the books and records of the publisher for a particular accounting statement at least once during the year following receipt of the statement. Watch out for what appear to be any unreasonable limitations on this right.

Indemnity

This is a legal term meaning that you're "insuring" the music publisher by promising to pay any damages they suffer if any of your *warranties* (promises and representations) about the song prove to be false or even if someone sues them making a claim that is "inconsistent" with those warranties. The two major areas publishers wish to protect against here are any claim that the song has infringed someone else's copyright and a claim that the music publishing rights are owned by someone else.

Although you may get a publisher to agree you are responsible only for *actual* breaches of your warranties regarding a song (for example, a breach proven by a final, nonappealable court decision), there is usually no negotiation of this clause. If, however, you've written only the music or only the lyrics to the song, make sure the indemnity only applies to your contribution. Otherwise you will be guaranteeing the promises of your co-writer for lyrics or music you did not write.

Disputes

What happens if there is a legal disagreement between you and the music publisher? You go to court, right? Right, but remember that if anyone sues anyone in this situation, it is most likely to be you suing the publisher for unpaid royalties, so this clause can be important. Also remember that legal actions are extremely expensive and time-consuming, so they are rarely an easy answer to any dispute. How can you make it easier and cheaper to sue a publisher if you need to?

First, try to get a specific provision that disputes will be resolved by binding arbitration under the rules of the American Arbitration Association. This will allow you to proceed much faster and with less expense to get a final, enforceable legal decision. Next, if you are dealing with out-of-state publishers, they will most likely require that disputes be resolved in their home state. If you live far from that state, try to get a provision that they can initiate any legal action against you in their state, but that if you initiate any action against them, it can be in your home state.

Most publishers will not agree to revisions in this area of their agreements, because they know you are more likely to sue them than they are to sue you, and they don't want to make it easy for you. Still, it's important to try to get these points anyway.

Co-Publishing and Participation Agreements

As I've mentioned throughout this book, bargaining power and negotiating strength can be wonderful things. Suppose you've had a few major recordings before you meet a particular publisher. Or suppose your song has had offers from a few different publishers. You may have the power to negotiate to keep some percentage of the music publishing ownership and income rights in addition to the songwriter's share of income I've discussed. This is often covered in a separate document that accompanies a single-song agreement, and it is commonly labeled a *co-publishing* or *participation agreement*.

A co-publishing share could be any percentage you agree upon. An equal co-publishing split would mean you equally own the copyright with the publisher, and that you would receive 50 percent of the normal publisher's share of income. As I discussed earlier in this chapter, in a music publishing agreement where you are transferring the *entire* publisher's share of income, the remaining songwriter's share will be 50 percent of the publisher's gross receipts from most outside sources. Therefore, an *additional* payment by the publisher to you of 50 percent of what would normally be the publisher's remaining share means you would end up with 75 percent of the publisher's gross receipts from most outside sources.

These are usually short, simple agreements. Though some of the same terms normally included in the single-song agreement are used in participation agreements, the main difference is in the computation of the co-publishing share. The usual formula would base your share on some definition of *net publishing receipts*. These might commonly be gross publishing receipts, allowing only deductions by outside companies not owned or controlled by the publisher, less the following:

1. the 50 percent share of receipts paid to you as a songwriter;
2. certain specific administration costs, such as copyright registration fees, the cost of demonstration recordings, and transcription costs for lead sheets; and
3. legal fees spent by the publisher for agreements or legal actions concerning the song (other than for any agreement or dispute between you and the publisher).

Some publishers also deduct an administration fee of 10 to 20 percent. As with administration fees imposed by publishers on standard single-song agreements, you should understand that this can substantially reduce the co-publishing income interest you thought you had. For example, if a publisher deducts a 15 percent administration fee from the net publishing receipts, your share of those receipts drops from 50 percent to 42½ percent. If you're forced to agree to this, at least insist that no deductions will be made for administration *costs* (including legal fees), because these are the costs the administration fee is designed to cover.

Co-Administration Agreements

With even greater bargaining clout, you might be able to require a co-administration agreement. Under this agreement, you and the publisher will each have the right not only to co-ownership of the copyright in your song, but to joint control over administration as well. This type of agreement usually gives both of you relatively equal rights to issue licenses for use of the song and collect money for those uses.

Co-administration agreements commonly contain the types of safeguard provisions discussed in chapter three relating to co-administration agreements between collaborators. For example, each of you might agree that only non-exclusive licenses can be issued without the approval of the other. Also, the agreement may require that neither of you can collect any money for the other, and that your income shares must be paid separately to each of you "from the source."

Administration Agreements

Suppose, with no help from anyone, you've gotten Sally Superstar to record your song. You might be able to obtain an agreement in which the publisher will deduct only 10 to 15 percent of gross receipts as an administration fee, giving you the rest. One negotiating point in this kind of agreement is whether or not the publisher can issue licenses without your consent.

Like normal single-song agreements, many administration agreements give complete power over the song to the publisher. These kinds of administration agreements are only different in that the percentage of income retained by the publisher is far lower, and the copyright ownership technically remains with the songwriter. In other administration agreements, the publisher only issues licenses with the approval of the songwriter. Another major point is that these agreements are for very limited periods of time (usually only three to five years).

You should be aware that most publishers who offer administration agreements will restrict their activities solely to administrative functions. They will not likely have the incentive to promote your song actively for any other uses when they have only a 10 to 15 percent interest. You could encourage them, however, by offering a larger percentage for cover recordings and other uses they obtain. For example, for those uses you could allow them a normal co-publishing share of 50 percent of the publishing share of income (which is the same as a 25 percent share of the gross income from the song).

━━━

Now you're ready to negotiate single-song agreements with music publishers! Remember, though, that this chapter is only intended to give you a general idea of major negotiating points for the common forms of agreement. A music industry attorney should still review the language of any document you will be signing, because one misplaced word can mean a world of difference to both your wallet and the safety of your rights.

CHAPTER 7

EXCLUSIVE SONGWRITING AGREEMENTS:
WRITING "ON STAFF"

What if a publisher likes so many of your songs that they want you to write just for them? They are likely to offer you an exclusive or *staff* songwriting agreement.

If your idea of a dream come true is to be paid every week to do nothing but write songs, that's exactly what staff writers do. They're hired by music publishers and paid weekly, monthly, or quarterly advances that are recoupable from their royalties (just as with single-song contract advances, no royalties are paid to you until the publisher recovers your advances from music publishing receipts that would otherwise be paid to you).

Exclusive agreements are also sometimes requested from songwriters in situations where no advances are offered. For example, a record company or record producer signing a songwriter/artist to an overall agreement may want to own and control all of the songs of that songwriter, even the songs that were written before the agreement took effect! Many of these "offers" include no advances. These types of agreements should be firmly negotiated, and you should continue to insist that you receive separate advances for these rights. You should also restrict this kind of agreement to your songs that are recorded and released under the record deal or production agreement.

Many publishers prefer to offer exclusive songwriter agreements to songwriters who are recording artists or record producers active with major record companies and projects, because they know there is a good possibility of a continuous source of recordings and income. The greater the past success of the songwriter/artist or songwriter/producer, the greater the likelihood of future income and the lesser the risk to the publisher, so most often these agreements involve only administration rights or co-publishing rights. The advances for such deals can be tremendous, as I'll cover later in this chapter.

The next category of individuals preferred by publishers for exclusive agreements are songwriters they believe have the potential to be major artists or producers. If you are in this category, negotiate for co-publishing on any of your songs that are first released featuring you or your group as the artist or producer.

An increasing number of music publishers sign potential recording artists with no intention of promoting any of the artists' songs for "outside" uses, focusing their efforts only on obtaining a recording artist agreement from a major record label. By involving themselves early in an artist's career, before the artist gains negotiating power, these publishers can obtain music publishing rights at a far lower price than they would have to pay after an artist becomes successful.

Despite the clear preference of many publishers for songwriters in the categories

> Many publishers prefer to offer exclusive songwriter agreements to songwriters who are recording artists or record producers active with major record companies and projects, because they know there is a good possibility of a continuous source of recordings and income.

described above, those of you who are not current or potential recording artists or producers are not without hope that you will ever be offered this kind of agreement. If a publisher is impressed by a substantial number of songs written or co-written by you, they may be interested in this type of agreement. If a publisher tests your writing skills by initiating collaborations with other songwriters signed to exclusive agreements with that publisher, or if a publisher gives you a writing assignment for submission to a specific artist, theatrical motion picture project, or television program, you are probably being considered for an exclusive agreement.

If you're offered this kind of agreement, and if you'll be paid reasonable advances for your songwriting services, and if music publishing is the primary business of the company you'll be writing for, you should probably consider the offer seriously. The following questions should help in determining whether an exclusive songwriting agreement is really for you.

> If a publisher tests your writing skills by initiating collaborations with other songwriters signed to exclusive agreements with that publisher, you are probably being considered for an exclusive agreement.

What Are the Advantages?

If the advance payments are enough to support you, you can quit your "other" job and write full-time. You'll probably discover substantial creative energy that was being drained elsewhere.

Additionally, you'll have full use of your publishers' resources to advance your career, because they want a return on their substantial investment in you. They'll work harder to get your songs recorded for records, theatrical motion pictures, and television programs, will introduce you to other talented songwriters, and will pay for sufficient studio time and personnel to produce high-quality demos.

What Are the Disadvantages?

For whatever songs you write during the term of the agreement, all of your administration rights, and possibly all of the music publisher's share of income rights, will be committed to the publisher for the life of the copyright in each song. In most exclusive songwriter agreements, whether or not you will be legally characterized as an *employee* of the publisher, the publisher will likely insist that all musical compositions you create during the term of the agreement will be works made for hire under U.S. Copyright Law.

One of the most significant disadvantages of an exclusive assignment of your administration rights and publishing income rights is that, for some artists, record producers, motion picture producers, and television producers, the unavailability of these rights will eliminate your songs from consideration for their projects. As I mentioned earlier, it's unfortunately a growing trend for many of these people to demand at least administration rights, if not all of the publishing rights, as a condition of using a song for their record, motion picture, or television program.

If you're a songwriter/artist looking for a record deal with a major label, however, an exclusive songwriter agreement should not pose any problem. Although some major labels want your music publishing rights as part of a record deal, this is usually negotiable, and most labels will not refuse to sign you as a recording artist based upon your pre-existing exclusive songwriting relationship with a publisher.

How Long Will You Be Committed?

Including all of the *option periods*, a term of three to five years is normal, because the publisher needs a year or two to develop your "value." An *option* means the publisher has the right to decide whether or not to renew your agreement for some additional period of time (usually, each option is for a one-year period). Try to limit the term to no more than four years.

How Much Will You Be Paid?

For songwriters with no previous major cuts or hits, you can expect advances (remember that these are fully recoupable from royalties), in the range of $200 to $500 per week for the first year, with increases of $50 to $150 per week in each additional year. This topic will arise quickly after a publisher decides to offer you an exclusive agreement, so be prepared to ask for enough to survive economically. In most negotiations, the publishers' first offer is likely to be lower than what they are prepared to pay you, so be ready to bargain with them!

For a writer with a string of major hits, a large publisher might pay recoupable advances of as much as $1,000 to $2,000 per week, so you may be able to negotiate increases based on success. For example, ask for a $200-per-week raise if any of your songs makes the top ten on the *Billboard* "Hot 100 Singles" or a $300-per-week raise if a song is a number one hit. One agreement I recently negotiated provided for a $10,000 bonus advance to the songwriter if any song reached the top 20 positions on the *Billboard*'s "Hot 100 Singles" chart.

What Other Payment Will You Get?

You always retain at least your songwriter's share of income, so after the publisher has recouped the advances and demo costs (usually one half of the total) paid on your behalf, the royalty structure is identical with that discussed earlier for single-song agreements. As with a single-song agreement, your writer's share should virtually never be less than 50 percent of the gross receipts (for most uses), unless you have co-written the particular song with another songwriter who will be entitled to a percentage of the writer's share.

What Effect Will This Type of Agreement Have on Songs You've Previously Written?

Some publishers will want all or some of these included as part of the deal. Others won't. If you have publishing rights available on songs that already earn income, an offer to transfer these rights as part of the "package" is a strong incentive for a publisher to sign you. If a publisher does request any of your *back catalog*, whether the songs are earning income or not, demand a separate payment for these songs, arguing that advances you'll be receiving are for future songwriting services. Also, insist on retaining co-publishing rights to these songs.

When signing a major songwriter/artist who is transferring copyrights for a string of pre-existing hit songs, it's not uncommon for a major publisher to require only administration or co-publishing rights and to pay a lump-sum, up-front advance well into the six-figure range. Just like an administration agreement for a single song, a typical exclusive administration agreement for a major artist would provide that the music publisher deduct 10 to 20 percent off the top from gross receipts, paying the entire balance to the songwriter.

If you have publishing rights available on songs that already earn income, an offer to transfer these rights as part of the "package" is a strong incentive for a publisher to sign you.

As to any songs written prior to the beginning of your exclusive songwriter agreement that you are *not* assigning to the publisher, remember to list these specifically on a *schedule* attached to the agreement. Otherwise, if you later exploit one of those songs on your own, the publisher may claim to own the rights under their agreement with you.

How Many Songs Must You Write?

Many publishers don't require a specific number. Others demand a certain total of "acceptable" songs per month or per year. If they insist on a minimum, make sure it sounds reasonable. Get them to agree that if they reject a song for purposes of the "quota," the publishing rights will *not* belong to them, and you'll be free to assign the publishing to anyone else for any rejected songs. This will discourage them from being too picky about which songs to accept. In one agreement I negotiated, the publisher was *required* to accept no less than one third of the songs submitted "in good faith" by the songwriter.

What If You Can't Write Enough Songs?

The publisher can usually terminate the agreement or elect not to exercise their option to keep you. What's worse, though, is that some publishers require the right to suspend advances to you until you write the minimum number of acceptable songs. This is a dangerous provision and should be severely limited. As long as you're submitting songs "in good faith," after two or three months of suspension, the agreement should terminate automatically if the publisher doesn't resume paying advances to you.

What About Reversion Clauses?

As I discussed in the last chapter, a reversion clause is a contractual provision that provides for a full return of all of your rights to a particular song or songs upon a certain event or the failure of a publisher to achieve a certain result. For songwriters without sufficient bargaining power, even for songs that were not recorded and released during the term of the exclusive agreement, it's usually difficult to get publishers to agree to any form of reversion after the deal is over. As I've already discussed, their position is usually that these were works made for hire under the U.S. Copyright Law, so they belong to the publisher for the life of the copyright. Publishers will also argue that they have taken a tremendous risk in paying you substantial sums over a long period of time, and that the retention of rights to your songs is fair compensation for that risk.

Even if you don't have much bargaining power, however, it might be possible to obtain a reversion of rights in unexploited compositions if you request the option to repay all unrecouped advances and demo costs at the end of the agreement. It's unlikely that you'll have that much money then anyway, but at least it leaves open the possibility of recovering your unexploited songs. As to *back catalog* you may have given to the publisher at the beginning of the agreement, there is little or no justification for a publisher's requirement that they retain the rights to unexploited compositions. Insist upon a reversion of rights to all songs from this category not commercially recorded and released during the term of the agreement, offering, if necessary, to repay any advance that was specifically designated for these songs.

What Happens to Relationships with Your Previous Collaborators?

This can be a sticky point. Publishers want some control over your choice of collaborators, because they want to prevent the creation of songs in which they will have only a small fractional interest. Some will permit you to write only with other staff writers signed to their company or signed to other major music publishers. Others require that you retain no less than a 50 percent interest in any co-written song, or that you promise to acquire for them the publishing rights of your collaborators. Try to obtain enough freedom to maintain your existing creative relationships, promising only to exert your "best efforts" to obtain your collaborator's publishing rights for your publisher.

An exclusive songwriting agreement can be a tremendous asset to a writer in need of regular income, connections, and demo facilities, although songwriter/artists close to being signed to a major record deal should generally wait to enhance their bargaining power. For those of you who are established, successful songwriters, whether or not you are also recording artists or record producers, these types of agreements should only be negotiated on the most favorable of terms.

CHAPTER 8

SONG PLUGGERS:
AN ATTRACTIVE ALTERNATIVE

What if you don't have the time or ability to promote your songs to artists, producers, record companies, and other users of music, but you don't want to deal with publishers who will require ownership and control in exchange for their services? Can you find someone else to promote your songs without having to give them too much power?

Independent Song Pluggers

The answer might be an independent breed of music professional often called a *song plugger*. Although the best professional managers of major music publishing companies are also known as song pluggers (many of whom are highly aggressive and adept at obtaining cover recordings), in this chapter, I'll discuss individuals who generally operate alone, without a staff and usually without even an office.

The strategies and techniques of independent song pluggers are the same as those used by the best major music publishers: They have to present the right song to the right person at the right time to get a particular recording. Some accomplish this through their personal network of friends and business acquaintances who are record producers, personal managers, recording artists, or television and motion picture producers. Others might be extremely talented detectives, aggressively uncovering information about potential recording projects, relentlessly pursuing whoever is in charge of making creative decisions for a particular project, and making sure an appropriate song is given to that person for consideration.

Fortunately for songwriters, in recent years there has been an increase in the number of independent song pluggers. It is therefore important to understand the advantages and disadvantages of business relationships with these people, as well as the kinds of agreements and *deal points* you should negotiate with them.

What Are the Advantages?
Many independent song pluggers do not require an assignment of your music publishing ownership and administration rights to do business with you. That leaves you free to reject any proposed use of your song. Under a normal music publishing agreement, depending on the wording of your reversion clause, a publisher might be entitled to all of the music publishing ownership and administration rights to your song just for obtaining a minor recording by an obscure recording artist in Ecuador.

Most song pluggers are content to receive merely an *income participation percentage* in your song for the cover recordings they obtain for you. Under this arrangement, the song plugger owns no portion of the copyright but merely receives a stated percentage of the income from the song. This income percentage, as you'll soon see, is usually lower than would be required from a regular music publishing company.

Some song pluggers are willing to operate on a nonexclusive basis, even for a single song. This allows you the advantage of continuing to promote your song on your own without any financial obligation to them for uses you obtain without them. Normal music publishers would almost never agree to this type of provision.

Most song pluggers do not ask to own or control the copyright to your song for one simple reason—they don't want to bear either the responsibility or cost of administration. To them, the higher income percentage and control are not worth the headaches and overhead expenses of a normal music publisher who produces demos, issues licenses, negotiates subpublishing agreements, collects money, and audits record companies for the accuracy of mechanical royalty payments. Therefore, due to the minimal expenses they incur in doing business, song pluggers are able to offer better financial terms to songwriters.

Some song pluggers are willing to operate on a nonexclusive basis, even for a single song. This allows you the advantage of continuing to promote your song on your own without any financial obligation to them for uses you obtain without them.

What Are the Disadvantages?

In contrast to most music publishing companies, song pluggers will probably not assist you in improving your songwriting skills or introduce you to new collaborators, and they will not pay for demos. Many are not as well connected to the motion picture and television industry as some of the major music publishers with affiliated companies in these areas. Additionally, *you* may have no desire to handle administrative chores for your songs either, and the idea of being a self-publisher (discussed in chapter nine) may not appeal to you in the least. As to the staff songwriting type of situation discussed in chapter seven, where you would be paid advances to write songs only for one company, a song plugger is unlikely to have either the money, the time, or the interest to handle this kind of deal properly.

If the areas described in the previous paragraph sound like your most pressing needs (or fears) right now, you will likely be better off finding a more traditional, full-service music publisher to work for you. If, however, you're relatively independent and can produce demos on your own, or if you want to attract interest in your songs on your own to improve your general clout and bargaining power in the music industry *before* you deal with major publishers, song pluggers might be a good alternative to consider. Even if the thought of handling your own music publishing administration scares you, once a significant use of one of your songs has been obtained, you can always retain a publishing company to handle the administration duties under the kind of administration agreement discussed in chapter six.

Song Plugger Agreements

Despite the intention of most song pluggers to avoid traditional music publishing responsibilities, some will still present you with a standard single-song publishing agreement identical to the one you would be given by a regular music publishing company. If the song plugger really has no experience or inclination to get involved in the traditional functions of copyright administration, you should propose an alternative to the standard single-song contract. More importantly, if you will be continuing to promote your song yourself, it is to your advantage to retain copyright ownership to preserve your bargaining power for later deals. At some point, a recording artist, a record producer, or a motion picture or television company may require all or part of your music publishing rights as a condition for a particular recording.

For most song pluggers, you should request an agreement in the general form of the participation agreements discussed in chapter six, with the exception that you will exclude the song plugger from any technical ownership of the copyright for the song involved. Under this arrangement, you will be transferring only certain potential income rights—not ownership or control.

What is the common range of these *income participation percentages*? Most song pluggers require either 10 to 25 percent of the gross income from a song or 20 to 50 percent of the music publishing share of income (see chapter six for a discussion of ways this share can be computed). Both of these formulas should be based on the income *you* receive from the song, leaving you free to continue offering your music publishing rights, if necessary, as a bargaining chip for further deals. You can compromise with a song plugger who demands an untouchable share of the music publishing income by agreeing that, if you transfer any portion of music publishing income to someone else, you will continue to pay the song plugger the same cash amount you would have paid if you had not made the transfer. In that situation, however, understand that if you later transfer *all* of your music publishing income to someone else, the song plugger's payment will come out of your normal songwriter's share of income. If you're not careful, you may end up keeping a smaller percentage of income from the song than anyone else!

In some song plugger agreements, even if you retain 100 percent of the exclusive administration rights, you might be asked to transfer a share of *passive* music publishing ownership rights (an ownership share without any right of control). Although you would still have sole power over licensing the use of the song and collecting the income, you would have no right to assign that portion of the copyright to anyone else. This situation is really just the traditional co-publishing deal described in chapter six, with the exception that you have retained all exclusive administration rights. As I discussed earlier, try to avoid *any* restriction on your future right to assign the entire copyright, because you should keep your bargaining options open as long as you possibly can.

Regardless of form or amount of income participation, try to insist that song pluggers only be paid for uses of the song obtained by them. Many song pluggers will agree to this, especially when you will be continuing to promote the song yourself.

For some areas of income, such as mechanical royalties from sales of records (discussed further in chapter nine on self-publishing), it is easy to differentiate a song's income from various sources for the purposes of this kind of nonexclusive agreement. For example, suppose a song plugger gets a recording by Sally Superstar, and you later get a recording of the same song by Bobby Bigshot. It will be easy to determine how much the song plugger is owed for the Sally Superstar recording, because you will receive separate mechanical royalty statements from the record companies for each of the artists.

The area of small performing rights poses a tougher problem, because for certain categories of small performances (most notably radio airplay), ASCAP and BMI (the two major societies making payments to songwriters and publishers for these rights) do not differentiate between different versions of the same song. For example, if the recording by Sally Superstar becomes a classic played by radio stations for many years, it is likely that small performing royalties for radio performances might still come from that record at the same time that the later version of the same song by Bobby Bigshot hits the airwaves. (This would not usually be a problem in other major areas of small performances. For example, prime-time network television performances of songs are identified with the title of the program and the air date).

> Most song pluggers require either 10 to 25 percent of the gross income from a song or 20 to 50 percent of the music publishing share of income.

There are various solutions to the problem of allocating performing rights income among various recordings. First, if the recording obtained by the song plugger is only an album cut and is never released as a featured, "A"-side single, there is little justification for granting any portion of radio performance income to the song plugger for that recording (although there may be an exception where the recording is commonly played on alternative music stations or album rock stations that often feature album cuts). If more than one recording of the song is frequently played on radio stations, you should devise some formula for payment. For example, the payment for the song plugger will be a fraction of the normal 10 to 25 percent payment, computed by the ratio between the total mechanical royalties received for the song plugger's recording against the total mechanical royalties received for all recordings of the song that are frequently played by radio stations.

Even for the nonexclusive representation arrangement described above, it would be fair to provide extra incentive for a song plugger to promote your material by agreeing that certain results will convert the deal into an overall income participation in all uses of the song. (This would also simplify the problem of separating the various income shares for different uses.) For example, if the recording obtained by the song plugger is the first major recording of the song, and if that recording becomes a top ten single on the *Billboard*'s "Hot 100 Singles" chart, you might agree that the song plugger's participation interest will apply to all uses of that song for the life of the copyright. The justification is that a first recording with that level of success usually creates a long-term value for the song.

If both of you will be promoting a song, of course, there's always the chance you will both submit the song to the same person or to different representatives of the same recording artist, motion picture producer, or television producer. In those situations, how do you determine who was responsible for a particular recording? One solution would be to agree to notify each other in writing of every submission of the song, any promises of use by anyone you've each contacted, or any *holds* (a promise that your song is being seriously considered for a particular use and a request that you not submit the song to anyone else while it's being held). The first person to submit that notice should be considered responsible for any cover recordings that result from the contact named in the notice.

After a song plugger has notified you that a particular person is holding or covering the song, the actual use of the song should ideally be required within six to nine months. Otherwise, a song plugger could theoretically be entitled to income forever by sending you a notice claiming that every major record producer, recording artist, motion picture producer, and television producer in town has received your song from them!

In all song plugger agreements, make sure it is understood that you are retaining all rights of ownership, administration, and control, and that you will have the right to reject any use proposed by the song plugger. As I've discussed, one of the disadvantages of standard music publishing agreements is the possibility you will be giving up substantial rights for a long period of time for only a minor use of your song.

As with any standard music publishing agreement, there should also be certain kinds of time limits in any deal with a song plugger. These are usually shorter than the reversion clauses discussed in chapter six for most single-song publishing agreements. If no commercial recording or hold has been obtained within three to six months, for example, you may want to terminate the song plugger's right to promote that song. If you've retained the song plugger for one particular project or "pitch" (for example, they are going to be eating lunch with Sally Superstar's manager next week and will present a tape of your song over dessert), you may want to make the time period even shorter.

Where Do You Find Good Song Pluggers?

These are very rare birds. They're certainly not in the telephone directory, and some of the people who might be best at song promotion may not even really see themselves as song pluggers. Many of these who *do* recognize their own abilities in this area and their value to songwriters might offer these kinds of services on a limited basis to only the very best songwriters.

A good song plugger could really be anyone with the right connections, a good ear for music, and the willingness to make the effort to promote your song to the right person. In fact, now that you know the general traits of song pluggers, you may be the first to suggest to someone that they should be one! Most typically, you might propose this arrangement to people who used to work for music publishing companies, record companies, personal managers, record producers, or particular recording artists. Virtually anyone who has experience and contacts in the music industry could be a good song plugger. It could even just be a friend outside the industry who has frequent social contact with many key industry people (or merely a contact with one key person connected closely to the recording artist you think would be perfect for your song).

> In all song plugger agreements, make sure it is understood that you are retaining all rights of ownership, administration, and control, and that you will have the right to reject any use proposed by the song plugger.

Now you know an alternative to the standard music publishing relationship that may be even better for your needs—a way to obtain professional promotion of your song in exchange for a limited income participation interest without losing ownership and control of your copyright. The next chapter will discuss in more detail the joys and perils of handling your own music publishing rights.

CHAPTER 9

SELF-PUBLISHING

What if you're the type of songwriter who isn't comfortable having someone else own and control your songs? What if you'd like to obtain your own cover recordings or find other uses of your music without having to give up any portion of your music publishing rights?

Although usually, at least at the beginning of your career, you will probably have to sign some type of music publishing agreement described in chapters six or seven to become successful as a songwriter, at some point you will have the option of keeping the rights to some songs for yourself. How do you handle your own administration? This chapter will cover the important aspects of self-publishing — the business of managing your own copyrights.

Deciding to handle the business side of your songwriting doesn't have to be an all-or-nothing proposition. For your worldwide hit single from Sally Superstar's smash album, you will probably save yourself a lot of headaches by just finding a major, worldwide music publisher to handle administration (the typical administration fees and form of agreement were discussed in chapter six). For a song that was only an album cut on a record with sales mostly in the U.S. or with limited foreign distribution in a few countries, it may be worth taking care of your own administration to save money. There are other situations where, for financial or other reasons, it might be better for you to retain total control over particular songs in your catalog.

The first step is to set up your own publishing company. Put your fears aside, because this is not a difficult process. No formal business organization is really needed, unless you have some special legal or financial reason to establish your company as a corporation or partnership. Discuss your plans with an attorney or accountant to be aware of the advantages and disadvantages of these common forms of business enterprise. Most likely, your company will merely be a *sole proprietorship*, which is just a technical term that says you're working for yourself!

In your particular town, city, or county, it may be technically necessary under the law to register your business name to legally start doing business under that name (before you do this, read the section in this chapter about *clearing* your name with a performing rights society). Many local laws also require the payment of some minimal business tax. Although your publishing activities will probably be conducted only through the mail, making you virtually invisible to local authorities, it is still smart to follow local licensing requirements. For reasons described in more detail in chapter ten, you want as much evidence as possible that you are conducting your songwriting activities as a business or profession. Establishing a checking account in the name of your business is a good practice for the same reason, and banks often require a business registration to open an account in the name of your company.

Now you're in business! You're a publisher! What do you do?

To recall the most basic principle of chapter one, you should first understand that until you assign or license any rights to your songs to someone else, *you* own and control all of the rights to your songs. (You might want to review the definitions of the various rights discussed in that chapter before reading further.) For anyone to use one of your songs for anything, they will need permission from you. In theory, at least, you can require any payment you want for any of these rights.

Mechanical Rights

These are the rights to mechanically reproduce a song on records, tapes, compact discs, and other recorded products. The first mechanical license you issue for your song is technically a *negotiated* mechanical license, which in theory is different from the *compulsory* mechanical license discussed in chapter one. As a practical matter, however, the major difference is that you can refuse requests for the negotiated license, holding your song for whatever artist you want to first record it. With the compulsory license, you have no choice—you cannot refuse someone's request to record your song.

In one important respect, both types of mechanical licenses are very similar: Virtually no record company will agree to pay you more for either license than the statutory rate for compulsory mechanical licenses (as this is written, 5¼ cents per song per copy sold). Many will try to insist upon a *three-quarter rate*, paying you 75 percent of the current statutory rate. You don't have to agree to this, but they may threaten (or bluff) that they will not record your song without a three-quarter-rate license.

Many record companies will send you *their* form agreement for a mechanical license, which is not usually drafted in terms most favorable to you. After you've received their license, if you feel major revisions are necessary, don't be afraid to request them. If the license seems generally unfair, don't be afraid to send them *your* standard license agreement for signature. In many cases, songs are produced and recorded, and records are pressed and released, before a record label bothers to have a mechanical license signed. In that situation, you have an extremely strong bargaining position to get what you want in your mechanical license, because a record company

> In many cases, songs are recorded and released before a record label bothers to have a mechanical license signed. In that situation, you have an extremely strong bargaining position to get what you want in your mechanical license.

will not pull records off the shelves and remove your song in order to get the contractual terms they want.

What's in a mechanical license? Compared to most agreements in the music industry, they're fairly simple. The major points include the identity of the record company and artist for which the license is being issued, the royalty rate, the due dates for accounting statements and payments (for example, quarterly or semiannually), and the required songwriter and music publisher credits that you want to appear on the record.

If a record company is using its own form of mechanical license, it will probably include a provision that allows the company to hold reserves of mechanical royalties. This will enable that company to withhold royalties that would otherwise be payable to you during a normal accounting period. The justification for this is that record companies distribute their products with a *return privilege*: Wholesalers and retailers can generally return some portion of the records they have purchased and get a refund of their money from the record company. In some situations, such as a brand-new act for which the record company can't accurately predict sales and return levels, the company may want to hold reserves of 50 percent or more. Try to limit the record company's right to hold reserves to no more than 25 percent of the mechanical royalties you would otherwise be owed.

Regardless of the level of reserves you agree upon, make sure that record companies must *liquidate* (pay to you) the money from each reserve they establish no later than one year after the date that particular reserve was first withheld. For example, if XYZ Records establishes a reserve of $2,500 in mechanical royalties for the quarterly accounting period January 1, 1990 through March 31, 1990, they should have to pay you any amount of that reserve that still remains on March 31, 1991.

Most major music publishers, as well as many small independents, use the Harry Fox Agency in New York City to issue mechanical licenses for them and collect mechanical royalties from record companies. That company will also conduct periodic audits of record company accounts when the circumstances are appropriate. If your songs have been covered on many albums, and if you think you will have trouble keeping track of all the various sources of mechanical royalties, it might be to your advantage to ask that company for a detailed description of their services and charges. They may be contacted at 205 E. Forty-second Street, New York, New York 10017, (212) 370-5330.

Synchronization Rights

These are the rights to synchronize a song with visual action for a television program, theatrical motion picture, home video device, or other filmed, taped, or reproduced visual action. The form of license you will issue to the user of your music (generally the production company of the program, picture, or video) will be a synchronization license.

As I discussed earlier in this book, many major motion picture and television producers will insist on a transfer of all or part of your music publishing rights as a condition of using your song in their production. It is important to understand that this is totally different from a synchronization license. In exchange for any transfer of ownership of your song, you should remember from chapter six to at least: (1) get a reversion clause that transfers your rights back to you if the song does not appear in the specified production, and if that production is either not released for general theatrical exhibition (this provision would be appropriate for movies), broadcast to the public (appropriate for television shows), or commercially distributed for sale to the public (videocassettes); and (2) require a payment for your publishing rights of no less than the amount you would have received for a synchronization license (it should ideally be a much greater amount, because you are also transferring ownership and control of your song).

The major points of a synchronization license include:

1. *The name of the party to whom you are issuing the license.* Later in the agreement you should specify that the company you are allowing to use your song cannot assign the license to anyone else. Suppose you've agreed to a low synchronization fee because you were told the movie was to be an independent production by a small company. If that company later allows a major motion picture company to purchase the script and music rights for development, you will be able to command a much higher fee for the use of your song.

2. *The name of the song being licensed.* I know this sounds obvious, but sometimes you might be licensing various musical *cues* and background music that don't really have names. Unless you are entering into an overall film score agreement where you will be composing all the music for a particular production (which is beyond the scope of this book), be sure to specifically identify whatever is being licensed. For example, you might only be composing and licensing four or five pieces of music for specific scenes, such as "thirty seconds of underscore for the chase scene in San Francisco."

3. *The name of the production for which the song will be used.* You don't want your music used for additional movies or programs unless you're aware of these uses in advance and have been paid an appropriate fee. For example, if your song is the theme of a hit motion picture, you should be paid another amount if the producers want to use the same song as the theme for the sequel to that movie. In another situation, you might have written the theme song for the "pilot" episode of a television program being considered for a possible series. You want to make sure that if the show does become a series, and if the producer wants your song to be the theme of the entire series, you will be paid an additional amount for those rights.

4. *The territory of the license.* In some circumstances, you may want to limit the license to only the United States or a specific foreign country or general territory. For example, for certain television commercials, a publisher might restrict the license only to Japan, because an association with a particular product might diminish the value of the song in the United States.

5. *The term of the license.* Most licensees will want to have the right "in perpetuity" (forever). For certain uses of songs, however, you may want to restrict the right to a limited period of time. For example, it is common practice to license songs for commercial use for limited periods of time (generally six months to a year). (This is different from writing a commercial jingle specifically for a sponsor. We might hear a specially written jingle for McDonald's or State Farm Insurance, for instance, for ten years or more.)

6. *The type of use being licensed and the rights being granted.* The money you

will be paid for the use of your song may vary greatly depending on the way in which it is used. That's why it's important, *before* you agree upon a price, to specify the way the song will be used. Will it be the theme throughout a movie? Or used over the opening or closing credits? Or only as "underscore" or background music? Or will it be a "featured" use, where characters in the production are singing or dancing while the song plays, or where the lyrics of the song substantially advance the story or explain a character's thoughts?

Whatever the use of your song in the production, the producer will usually also want the right to use it for advertising and promotion of the production. This should normally be acceptable, unless you think you are being paid too little to allow this use of your song.

If appropriate, make sure the license is expressly *nonexclusive*. This means you can license the song to someone else for another production. An exclusive license would be appropriate if you are being paid to use your song as the theme song to a television series. In such a situation, though, it is likely that production companies would insist upon ownership and control of your copyright, because they will want your song to become identified *only* as the theme to their shows, and they won't want you issuing licenses to anyone else for any purpose at all.

7. *The money being paid for the license.* These amounts are far from standard and vary greatly, depending upon factors such as the way your song is used, the budget of the picture, and the bargaining power of your song based on its past success. Some small motion picture and television production companies might offer close to nothing for a synchronization license, promising you that your song will gain great exposure and will earn performance royalties from ASCAP or BMI.

A minor, background use of ten or twenty seconds of music in a major motion picture might be worth as little as $200 to $500, although *any* identifiable portion of a hit song will command a substantially higher price. A relatively prominent use of a song in a major motion picture might generate a synchronization license fee in the range of $2,500 to $20,000, with even higher amounts likely to be offered for the use of a classic hit as a title theme. If a superstar songwriter/artist is being asked to specially create a theme song for a movie, the fee could be as high as $50,000 or more for a single song!

The synchronization fees for television are substantially lower, primarily because the production budgets for television are far lower than those for major motion pictures. Even for the prominent use of a hit song in a music-oriented show like *Miami Vice*, the synchronization fee is likely to be no higher than $3,500 to $5,000. For most television shows, especially those that will not be broadcast in prime time over network television stations, the fees will be much less. If a writer is hired to write a new theme song for a television show, the payment will be in the range of $1,500 to $20,000, depending upon the clout of the songwriter and the music budget for the show.

Regardless of the synchronization use for which you're licensing your song, it's always best to require some payment up front, because there are never any guarantees that you will earn any other money from the production in question. ASCAP and BMI performance royalties, as you'll soon see, are only earned

It's important, *before* you agree upon a price, to specify the way the song will be used.

from certain specific types of performances and from certain surveys of performed songs. In the case of theatrical motion pictures that are never shown on television and are not distributed outside the United States, for instance, it's likely that the use of your song in that picture will earn no performance royalties at all.

Sometimes you can get a producer to agree to pay you some cents-per-copy rate on sales of videocassettes, videodiscs, or other versions of a motion picture that will be sold for home use. This is very difficult, however, because most of these companies do not like to share their profits from these types of sales. If you *can* get a royalty, however, there are at least two formulas you could reasonably propose.

First, you can ask for a normal mechanical royalty rate, just like you would receive for the mechanical reproduction of your song on records, tapes, or compact discs. The other formula would be for you to be paid a "pro rata" share of 5 or 6 percent of the wholesale price of the video product. Some companies will agree to allocate this percentage to all of the music in a movie, although it's usually only applied for a movie in which music was a major part of the production. You compute your share by one of two fractions.

In one fraction, you make the numerator (the upper number of the fraction) the number of minutes during the movie that your song was playing and the denominator (the lower number of the fraction) the total number of minutes of music in the movie. Unless your song was played throughout the movie as a recurring theme or was a very long song, this is probably *not* the formula to choose. The other formula would use the number "1" for the numerator (representing your song) and the total number of songs in the movie for the denominator. So if there are fifteen songs in the movie, you would receive $\frac{1}{15}$ of 6 percent of the wholesale price for all video products sold that embody the movie that uses your song.

Print Rights

These are the rights to print sheet music and other printed reproductions of your song. Compared to the money generated by mechanical royalties, small performance royalties, and synchronization license fees, this is a far smaller segment of the music publishing industry.

Most activity in print music is confined to major hits that have been at (or very near) the top of the charts, standards that have remained popular through the years, and songs that appear on major albums by major artists. The most common forms of print music are:

1. single-sheet music copies for piano/vocal or other instruments;
2. full orchestrations for high school, college, and professional bands and orchestras;
3. folios that include a variety of major hits by different artists and songwriters;
4. personality folios that include major hits of the same artist or songwriter or songs from a particular album of an artist; and
5. educational folios of songs for instructional purposes.

It's both expensive and difficult for an independent publisher to print and effectively distribute print music copies, so most publishers assign this function to companies that specialize in this area. You can find their names by examining the print music credits for the "Hot 100 Singles" chart in *Billboard* magazine.

The major points of negotiation for agreements with print music companies include the following:

The Advance

For an entire album, this should be in the range of $15,000 to more that $60,000, depending upon the importance of the artist performing the song. For a single song, it's possible to receive an advance of $1,500 to more than $5,000.

The Royalties

As this is written, the common licensing fees you can expect to receive for these uses will fall in the following ranges: (a) for sheet music, fifty to sixty cents per copy or 20 percent of the retail price; (b) for orchestrations, songbooks, and folios, 12½ percent of the retail price (which for songbooks and folios will be computed "pro rata" by the ratio between your song and the total number of songs in the printed edition); and (c) for print music products used primarily for educational purposes, 10 to 20 percent of the retail price.

The Term

Like subpublishing and administration agreements, your print music agreement should have a term of only three years. If the advance paid to you is high enough, print music companies may insist on a longer period. They will also want an inventory *liquidation* period during which they may continue to sell their existing stock after the end of the deal. This should range from six months to one year.

Commitments

Like a reversion clause in a single-song agreement, this provision forces print companies to actually perform in a specified manner. If, for instance, they don't print and distribute sheet music copies of your song for sale to the public within thirty days after the song enters *Billboard*'s "Hot 100 Singles" chart, the print rights should revert to you automatically. Some companies will not agree to this kind of requirement.

Print music is an extremely specialized area. If you have a song being recorded by a major artist, or even a new artist on a major label, it may be appropriate for this kind of exploitation, and you should contact print music companies for possible interest.

Small Performing Rights

These are distinguished from other performing rights primarily because the major performing rights societies (ASCAP and BMI) collect these sums for their songwriter and publisher members. (SESAC, another performing rights organization, collects a far smaller portion of performing rights payments than does ASCAP or BMI.) As I discussed earlier, small performances mostly include performances on radio, on television, in motion picture theatres outside the U.S., in nightclubs, in concert halls, and in commercial stores.

It's crucial to join a performing rights society if your songs will be performed in any manner that might generate a payment. Unless you have only licensed your song for a limited, local performance where one fee covers all rights to use the song (including performance), it will be impossible for you to license your small performing rights yourself across the country (or the world) and collect money for the performances. It's important to understand, though, that these organizations *only* collect sums for a specific area of income from the use of your songs. *They are not publishers or copyright administrators, and they are not responsible for collecting money for any other use of your songs.*

You should contact the performing rights organization of your choice to find out about membership. It's fairly easy to join as a songwriter. If you also want to join separately as a publisher for your own songs, you must join the same organization to which you belong as a songwriter. If you are publishing the songs of some other songwriter who belongs to another performing rights organization (for example, one of your collaborators), you can establish a separately named publishing company with the performing rights organization of which that songwriter is a member.

If you can qualify with one of the performing rights organizations as publisher member, be sure to *clear* the name of your publishing company before you register it as a business, because they may already have a publisher member with a name identical to yours. Once they've approved your name, they will "hold" that name for a limited period of time until you complete the process of joining as a publisher member.

Always check with the performing rights organization you prefer as to its current qualifications for membership. Generally, though, you should be able to join as a publisher or songwriter if:

1. a record has been released with your song as one of the cuts; or
2. your song has been performed as part of a television program or motion picture (as long as you can obtain *cue sheets* from the producer to prove the song was included in the production); or
3. your song has been performed as part of any radio show (here you will need a radio station *log sheet* as proof of the performance); or
4. your song has been performed in any other manner covered within the performing rights normally licensed by the organization you are joining (as long as you have proof of the performance).

Actually, even if you can't join as a full member, there may be a provision allowing you to become an associate member of one of the organizations. Also, if you're only trying to join as a songwriter, it may be sufficient that you've had a song signed to a music publishing company that is a member of the performing rights organization. It's generally easier to become a songwriter member than a publisher member.

Despite the technical description of categories included in small performing rights, the vast majority of the money paid for performances of music results from radio and television performances in the United States. It would be impossible (or at least financially prohibitive) for the performing rights societies to monitor and log every performance of every song on every radio and television station in the country.

The vast majority of the money paid for performances of music results from radio and television performances in the United States.

Therefore, each of them has a different system for calculating payments for performances of your song. These are highly complex methods of monitoring (or surveying) performances, and you should discuss the details with representatives of the organization of your choice.

It's also important to understand the procedures for registering and indexing your songs with the organization you join. Otherwise, they will not be able to recognize and log performances of your song and calculate the payment owed to you.

In the area of records, performing rights organizations must be informed when the record is released. For motion pictures and television programs, they will need cue sheets that give details about the name of song, the name of the picture or program, the type of use, and the number of minutes of use. These factors can all affect the amount of payment. If you are requesting that a performing rights organization make some payment to you for performances of your song on local or syndicated television (if the performances are not picked up on any survey), cue sheets from the program's producer or log sheets from a local television station can help you present your case.

How much income can you make from small performing rights? If you have a number one hit that is a *crossover* success on more than one record chart (for example, pop, R&B, and adult contemporary), depending upon how many weeks it stays at the top of the charts, you might earn an extra $200,000 to $500,000 as the combined songwriter's and publisher's shares of small performance income from radio alone. A number one hit on the country chart that does not appear on the pop or adult contemporary charts might earn in the range of $75,000 to $150,000 in combined songwriter/publisher small performance income from radio airplay. These dollar amounts are only estimates. Your song could earn far less or far more, and any song that becomes a "standard" will continue to earn money for many years.

For many songs, the licensing of small performing rights creates the largest source of income, so the importance of these rights and the role of the performing rights societies in collecting and distributing performing rights payments can be critical to your financial success. When granting licenses, you should therefore be careful not to give away any rights that may weaken both the right of your performing rights organization to collect money on your behalf and your own right to be paid for these uses of your music.

This problem appears commonly today in synchronization licenses that allow *source licensing*. For motion picture and television producers, the right to grant a *source license* allows them to give a television station (or anyone else) permission to perform the music as part of a producer's movie or television program without that station having to make any payment to songwriters, music publishers, or their performing rights societies. Source licenses are very rare now, but they may someday become common.

Independent television stations have been seeking this type of license for a long time. They claim they pay enormous sums to production companies for the rights to broadcast television shows and movies, and that they should have the right to perform the music in the program or movie for the same price. They therefore want to obtain their music performance licenses from the "source" of the program, not from songwriters, music publishers, or performing rights societies. (A license from a music publisher to a television station for the performance of music would be referred to

> For many songs, the licensing of small performing rights creates the largest source of income, so the importance of these rights and the role of the performing rights societies in collecting and distributing performing rights payments can be critical to your financial success.

as a *direct license*.) This issue is so important that these independent stations have pursued this argument in court and in Congress for over thirty years — so far without success.

For many years, most television stations have obtained the right to perform *all* of the music licensed by ASCAP and BMI through the payment to each organization of an annual, *blanket license* fee based on a particular station's income. This type of fee was initially devised for two reasons. First, far too much paperwork would be involved in issuing a separate music performance license for every television program and motion picture. Second, the blanket license was initially considered a *less expensive* alternative to granting individual performance licenses for every song.

If source licensing of television programs and motion pictures for independent television stations ever becomes standard procedure, songwriters and music publishers will be unlikely to receive nearly the same amount for small performing rights from this use as they now earn under the present system of collection. This is because they are usually in a weak negotiating position when dealing with motion picture and television producers, and it's impossible to imagine these companies paying music publishers and songwriters the amounts now being collected by performing rights societies from independent television stations. Songwriters, music publishers, and their performing rights societies will therefore continue to do everything in their power to oppose source licensing.

Despite the fact that motion picture and television producers are now asking for the right to grant source licenses, they are *also* opposed to converting the present system entirely to one of source licensing. They realize that under source licensing, songwriters and publishers will not receive extra money from television stations for performing rights, and that they will then demand higher licensing fees as a condition of placing a song in a particular production. Even though producers will certainly refuse to match the amounts songwriters and music publishers would have earned through the ASCAP/BMI collection systems, they will still have to pay substantially more for music than previously. Also of importance, now that many producers are music publishers themselves, they want to protect the extra income *they* now receive from performing rights revenues.

Motion picture and television producers are taking steps today to protect their interests if the independent television stations ever win the argument over source licensing. First, a far greater number of producers are now requiring a total assignment of music publishing rights as a condition of recording a song for use in a production. *They* will then be in the sole position to determine who will perform the music and on what terms. Whether or not source licensing ever becomes prevalent, they will never be restricted in their ability to exploit their productions. Second, those producers who don't require a transfer of music publishing rights *do* demand the right, in their synchronization license agreements, to license all performances of the songs in their productions for no additional sum. If performing rights societies are ever forbidden to license these rights and collect money for the performances, the motion picture and television producers will be able to grant these performance licenses.

For the reasons I've discussed, source licensing would be a financial disaster for songwriters. If the independent television stations win their battle, many observers believe that radio stations and network television stations won't be far behind in

> Motion picture and television producers are taking steps today to protect their interests if the independent television stations ever win the argument over source licensing.

claiming they shouldn't pay for performing rights either! Songwriters *must* take steps to protect themselves against source licensing.

Be sure in your synchronization licenses to at least try to include language stating that the producer cannot license performances of your song to any television station that is not licensed by your performing rights organization, unless that television station contacts you directly for a performing rights license (a direct license). This may be difficult to get from some motion picture and television production companies for the reasons I've mentioned, but you must at least make the effort.

If you ever read anything about pending legislation on *any* issue in Congress involving television stations and the licensing of music, it's probably related to source licensing. Contact your representatives in the Senate and the House of Representatives, and let them know your views. Otherwise, someday the most significant area of music publishing income will evaporate, and only songwriters who are successful recording artists will earn enough income to survive.

Grand Performing Rights

This term is most often applied to the dramatic performance of music in musical plays. It is also generally viewed as the right to dramatically perform a song in a manner that advances the plot or story line of a production (whether a movie or TV program). As a practical matter, the dramatic performance of songs in a theatrical motion picture or television production (for example, a motion picture like *Fiddler on the Roof* or a television program like *Fame*) usually generates separate small performing rights payments. The grand performing right in these kinds of programs is most often covered in the fee paid for the synchronization right for the song.

If a musical producer wants to use one or two or your songs for a play, negotiate for a weekly fee. You might charge $50-$200 per week per song for performances of the play in small theaters, regional theaters, dinner theaters, or other theaters not considered "first-class" theaters by the Dramatist's Guild. (The Dramatist's Guild is headquartered at 234 W. Forty-fourth Street, New York, New York, 10036, 212-398-9366. It is the major organization governing negotiations for composers and authors of major dramatic and musical productions in the United States.) For large legitimate theaters in major cities, when your song is used prominently in a musical, you might try to charge $500 to $1,500 per week per song. The rates suggested in this paragraph should be charged for *each* theater where the musical is being performed.

If you are writing substantially all of the music or lyrics for a musical play, you should not agree to accept a mere weekly licensing fee, and you should not sign standard single-song agreements for all of the songs with the producer of the show. The best practice in that situation would be to start with the basic form of agreement recommended by the Dramatist's Guild. It's called the "Dramatist's Guild Approved Production Contract for Musical Plays." The "APC" is quite long and complex, but it should serve as the starting point for your negotiations, because it will provide for payment to you of a percentage of the profits of the play. This is the only area of activity in the music industry where it is common, accepted practice for virtually all songwriters (regardless of bargaining power) to be entitled to a profit participation percentage from a production (only if they've written substantially all of the music or lyrics for the play).

Derivative Rights

These are the rights to create other works derived from your song. These might include foreign lyrical translations, new foreign lyrical versions, or a movie, television program, television commercial, or play based upon a song or its title.

If you have a major hit song and someone wants to use your song in a commercial ad campaign, you could probably command a payment of $100,000 to $300,000 or more for a six-month to one-year license. For a commercial using a classic hit from a classic artist (like the Beatles), the amount could be even higher. For these payments, an advertiser will usually want the right to change the song's lyrics to suit the product.

If you retain a lyricist to create a foreign translation of the English language lyric of your song, offer a flat fee of a few hundred dollars. If the lyricist demands a percentage, keep it in the range of a 10 to 15 percent share of your normal songwriter's royalties for the song. If a lyricist will be creating a totally new foreign lyric version of your song, expect to pay as much as 25 to 50 percent of the songwriter's share of royalties in the countries where the new lyric version is exploited.

Sometimes a motion picture or television program is based upon the story line of a song, such as the "Ode to Billie Joe." In this situation (again assuming you have a major hit song), the licensing fee will usually be in the same range as that for a commercial ad campaign but should also include a participation in the profits from the picture.

In other instances, a picture or program might use only the title of a song that makes viewers *think* of the song. The producers of the movie *Rhinestone* (which starred Dolly Parton and Sylvester Stallone) made a payment to the copyright owners of the song "Rhinestone Cowboy," even though song titles are *not* protected under copyright law, and it is normally difficult to protect the use of titles. The motion picture *Baby, It's You* (which starred Roseanna Arquette) was named after a song title and used the song as a recurring theme in the soundtrack.

Foreign Rights

Even for those of you who choose the independent route and act as your own publishers, if you have a song being actively exploited in a foreign country or general region, it will probably be best to enter into a subpublishing agreement for that country or territory. Foreign subpublishers will be far more efficient in collecting the amounts due for the use of your song in their areas, because they will be expert in the customs and practices of their national performing rights societies and mechanical collection societies, as well as local tax laws and other restrictions that may apply to your income. Also, you will generally collect more money if you deal directly with a foreign subpublisher than if you collected foreign royalties through a U.S. publisher, because you have eliminated the percentage taken by the domestic publisher.

Despite these common advantages of direct subpublishing agreements, in a situation where you have a worldwide hit by a major recording artist, it's probably best just to obtain a worldwide administration agreement from a major U.S. publisher. You can then take advantage of all of its pre-existing subpublishing arrangements around the world. Otherwise, you will have to negotiate far too many different subpublishing agreements, and you may have trouble keeping track of all of the different subpublishers and their obligations to you.

If you decide a direct subpublishing agreement would be best for you in a particular situation, the key areas of negotiation are the same as for a single-song agreement, but your negotiating demands will be entirely different. The major areas of negotiation in a foreign subpublishing agreement are as follows:

The Legal Rights to Be Transferred

As I discussed earlier, in a regular single-song agreement in the United States with a publisher, you assign all rights of ownership and control to that publisher. In a foreign subpublishing agreement, *you* retain technical ownership and grant only certain specified, restricted rights to the subpublisher for a specific territory. These normally include the standard rights to grant licenses for mechanical reproduction, synchronization, performance, print, and translations, but the big difference is that most of these licenses will require your approval. Be especially sure that you retain approval over any cover recordings of your song. In this sense, the subpublisher is more like your agent in a foreign country.

Virtually all subpublishers will want the rights you grant to be exclusive in their territory, as they will not want another music publisher exercising rights to the song. Remember, though, that subpublishers are really your agents, and that *you* remain the owner of the copyright. Therefore, unlike a normal single-song publishing agreement in the United States, you should *not* give them the right to refuse your request for a particular use of your song. In subpublishing agreements, you should reserve the right to exercise all of the rights you've granted to the subpublisher yourself, with the condition that the subpublisher will collect its normal share of income from any use in its territory. For example, you should have the separate right to authorize the performance of your song in a motion picture that will be exhibited in the subpublisher's territory or the separate right to license your song for a television commercial.

The Advance

These are seldom as large for foreign subpublishing agreements as for agreements in the United States, because no country in the world has as large a music market as we do (in terms of dollars spent). The size of your subpublishing advance will depend upon the subpublisher's prediction of your song's financial success in the territory covered by the agreement. If your song has been included on an album of an obscure artist with no prior sales history anywhere in the world, you may be offered no advance at all.

Term of the Agreement

These types of agreements are usually for three to five years. You may want to grant a possible extension period of two years if the subpublisher has successfully promoted your song for cover recordings. For instance, you may provide a strong incentive for the subpublisher by offering an extension of the deal if the subpublisher obtains at least two cover recordings you approve during the initial term.

Territory

Try to limit this as much as possible to the particular territory in which the recording of your song is being released or in which the subpublisher conducts most of its

In a foreign subpublishing agreement, *you* retain technical ownership and grant only certain specified, restricted rights to the subpublisher for a specific territory.

business. Certain countries are usually lumped together in one territory for sub-publishing purposes (for example, Germany, Austria, and Switzerland). Avoid agreeing to a worldwide deal based upon one release in one country.

You should be aware that the sale of your song on recorded products manufactured in any country of the European Economic Community (mostly Western Europe) presents special problems. This is because the laws of the EEC forbid restrictions on the "free flow of goods" across national boundaries of its member countries. Therefore, if you give music publishers agreements limiting their collection rights to only one country, you may be limiting their power to collect royalties efficiently for products shipped from that country and sold in another country. There are currently agreements being negotiated between the mechanical collection societies and performing rights societies of the EEC countries that may solve this problem. This will be a continuously evolving issue in the years to come, however, and it may someday be simplest and most efficient to always have one publisher handle copyright administration for all countries in the EEC.

Royalties and Other Payments

The most common split will be 25 percent to the subpublisher and 75 percent to you, although 80-20 and 85-15 splits are not unreasonable for the right song. If you or your song have extremely strong bargaining power, you might be able to require as high as a 90 percent share for yourself.

It's common to offer a sliding scale to subpublishers based upon cover recordings they obtain with your approval. For example, in the 75-25 situation, you could offer to split 60-40 for cover recordings in the territory that you approve.

Disputes

If you have a legal dispute with a subpublisher in a foreign country, it will probably be extremely difficult and expensive to pursue your claim. Insist in your agreement that the subpublisher consent to the jurisdiction of the federal courts located in your state for the resolution of any disputes concerning your subpublishing agreement.

■■■■

Now you know what it takes to be your own publisher. You can also see why many songwriters find some other company to tackle the complex business problems of copyright administration for their songs!

CHAPTER 10

USING THE TAX LAWS TO YOUR ADVANTAGE:
SOME BASICS

Let's face it. You don't like to do your taxes—nobody does. Whether you work many long hours to figure out you owe the government more money, or you work many long hours to figure out the government owes you money, it's still usually an exhausting, difficult job.

A lot of you probably take what you think is the "easy" road to figuring taxes—you pay accountants, attorneys, or storefront tax preparation services to handle the whole mess. Unfortunately, the easy road might also cost you much more than merely the fee you pay for the service, because many of the people who prepare taxes for you will have no adequate understanding of all the tax principles that apply to songwriting, and you will pay the government more than you really owe.

For those of you who don't fall prey to mistaken counseling from financial advisors, your own lack of knowledge of key tax laws or fear of an audit by the IRS may cause you to waste significant amounts of money every year by failing to take legitimate deductions to which you are entitled—money that could be better spent on purchasing musical equipment or producing demonstration recordings of your songs. Whether you prepare your own taxes or hire someone else to do the work for you, it's critical to understand at least the basics, so this chapter will discuss general federal tax principles that affect your activities in the music industry. I will also discuss generally the relationship between federal tax regulations and those of many states, although you should always seek professional help in your own state to be sure you are complying with the proper laws.

This chapter will *not* go into detail concerning specific federal tax code sections that might cover your songwriting, because many tax laws and regulations are changed quite frequently, and that kind of discussion could be useless and out-of-date by the time you read this book. There are, however, certain general principles that have remained fairly constant over the years. After reading this chapter, you should at least know the proper questions to ask your accountant or other tax advisor, as well as the major areas to investigate, review, and revise if you think you are paying too much.

Let's start with the most basic principle of tax law that might apply to you—tax deductions. If your songwriting is a *trade* or *business* (which I'll discuss later), any deductions that you are legally allowed to take for expenses incurred in pursuing your songwriting activities will reduce your *other* income for purposes of computing the taxes you owe. For example, if you're making $25,000 per year in commissions from your job selling real estate, you might owe $4,750 in taxes. (This is just a hypothetical situation, as the actual taxes due at this income level might be some other amount, depending on what other deductions, exemptions, or credits you might have.) Now let's suppose you have $7,500 in songwriting expenses that are legally deductible. Your taxable income would be reduced to $17,500, and your taxes would be computed based on *that* amount.

Depending on the size of your deductions, the *percentage* of your income you owe for taxes might also be reduced. For example, at the $17,500 income level, your taxes might be only $2,625 (which is a smaller percentage of $17,500 than the percentage of $25,000 that $4,750 represents). You've just saved almost $3,000! (Again, all of the numbers and percentages I've used are only for generally illustrating the principle of tax deductions and the way they affect your taxes. Tax brackets are changed every few years by Congress, so a detailed example of income levels and actual tax bracket percentages from the IRS tax table would probably be accurate only on the day I wrote this chapter.)

There's another general principle of tax law called a tax *credit*. At present, it doesn't appear that any significant tax credits are available to songwriters, but you should understand what they are in case someday the law changes to provide one for you.

A *tax credit* is a direct reduction in your tax liability, rather than a reduction of your income for the purpose of computing taxes. In the example above (a $25,000 income level, with a tax of $4,750 owed), if you had a $7,500 tax *credit*, rather than a $7,500 tax *deduction*, your gross income would still be considered $25,000, but you would not owe any income taxes at all! The $7,500 tax credit would be subtracted directly from the amount of your tax liability, not from your gross income.

Obviously, tax credits save you a lot more money than tax deductions. That's why they are made available only under special laws or regulations passed by Congress and intended to favor certain kinds of investment (for example, investments in equipment for solar power have been allowed tax credits in recent years). It used to be that you could generally take a tax credit up to 10 percent for any type of investment in equipment used in your *trade or business*, but that tax credit provision was basically removed from the law in 1986. Under that law, if you bought a $10,000 piece of musical equipment, you might have been able to use $1,000 as a tax credit for the tax year during which the equipment was purchased. Perhaps someday Congress will again make this credit generally available for investments in equipment used in a trade or business. (There are other ways, however, to take deductions for instruments

If your songwriting is a *trade* or *business*, any deductions that you are legally allowed to take for expenses incurred in pursuing your songwriting activities will reduce your *other* income for purposes of computing the taxes you owe.

and recording equipment used in your songwriting activities that will be discussed later in this chapter.)

Is Your Songwriting a Trade or Business? Or Merely a Hobby?

Now that I've introduced you to the term *trade or business*, it's critical that you understand the importance of that term to *any* type of tax deduction or tax credit you think may be available to you. Unless you're conducting your songwriting activities as a trade or business under the rules of the IRS, your songwriting will be considered a hobby, and you will only be able to deduct your expenses to the extent of your gross receipts from songwriting.

You must attempt to avoid having your songwriting classified as a hobby, then, because if you're losing money as a songwriter, your losses will not be deductible from income you receive from other occupations. In the first example I used for explaining tax deductions ($25,000 in gross income from real estate sales, $4,750 in taxes due, and $7,500 in songwriting expenses), if your songwriting is considered by the Internal Revenue Service to be a hobby, *none* of the expenses would reduce either your gross income or your taxes due. You would have to actually earn money from songwriting to take any deduction at all. For example, if you received $2,000 in music publishing income in addition to your $25,000 from real estate sales, $2,000 of your $7,500 in songwriting expenses would be allowed as a tax deduction to reduce your taxable income.

If you regularly make a profit from your songwriting activities (that is, where your income for a particular year exceeds your expenses), that's the easiest way to qualify your songwriting as a "business or profession." The law used to provide that, if a particular activity was profitable for you in two out of five consecutive tax years, you were *presumed* to be engaging in the activity as a trade or business. The advantage of this type of presumption is that it places the burden of proof on the IRS to establish that you're *not* in a trade or business. As of the date this chapter is written, it has become slightly more difficult to gain the benefit of this legal presumption, because profitability for a given activity (like your songwriting) is now required in *three* out of five consecutive years.

Unfortunately, the presumption described above misleads some attorneys and accountants who handle songwriters to "play it safe," reviewing only income and profit to determine whether a songwriter is in a trade or business. They mistakenly advise their clients that if they don't make a profit for the required number of years, they cannot claim to be engaged in a trade or business. Others give equally incorrect advice, counseling *anyone* who is spending more than they earn that their music-related write-offs are limited by the amount of their income from music-related activities.

Both types of well-meaning (but misinformed) practitioners cost songwriters tremendous amounts of money that should have been legal, justifiable write-offs — money that could be much better spent on your career. They mistakenly convince songwriters not yet earning any income to believe they cannot deduct anything. The impact is greatest on those of you with another profession that pays well, who could be significantly reducing your taxes for that primary source of income.

Whether or not you earn a profit (or any money at all) from your songwriting

---

Unless you're conducting your songwriting activities as a trade or business under the rules of the IRS, your songwriting will be considered a hobby, and you will only be able to deduct your expenses to the extent of your gross receipts from songwriting.

activities is only one factor the IRS may consider in determining whether your efforts will be classified as a hobby or as a trade or business. Under the law, a taxpayer is considered as engaging in an activity as a trade or business, rather than a hobby, if the activity has been entered into and carried on in good faith for the *purpose* of making a profit. A reasonable expectation of profit is not necessarily required, but the facts and circumstances must indicate a profit motive and objective. Of course, the longer someone engages in a business activity without generating income or making a profit, the more likely the IRS will audit the return and require the taxpayer to prove the existence of a trade or business. This prospect should not, however, discourage you from taking the deductions you rightfully deserve.

There are many factors taken into consideration in determining your intention to make a profit. Some that you should especially utilize include the following:

1. *The manner in which the activity is carried on.* Keep organized records of your activities in the music industry. Open a separate checking account for expenses, maintain a mileage log of all travel for business purposes, retain copies of all business-related correspondence sent or received. Use a special diary or calendar to record all engagements and appointments. These "habits" all help establish that you are conducting yourself as a business.

2. *The expertise of the taxpayer and the taxpayer's advisors in the taxpayer's field of activity.* Keep track of any educational programs you've taken to improve your musical and songwriting skills. This doesn't necessarily mean courses at Julliard. Various programs conducted by songwriter organizations and local schools can be important, as can private instruction. Also, be sure to consult with specialists in the music field, whether accountants or attorneys, at every appropriate opportunity. In one tax case many years ago that found a musician to be in a business or profession, a major determining factor was that he had formalized his business relationships with written agreements drafted by a music industry attorney.

3. *The time and effort spent by the taxpayer in carrying on the activity.* In order to establish that you engage in songwriting as a business, it's also critical to prove that you conduct your activities on a regular basis. If you only write songs alone, once a month, and send a demo tape once every two months, an IRS auditor might have good reason to question your motives and determine you wrote songs for a hobby. On the other hand, it would be hard to challenge your claim of a trade or business if you can establish that you write or co-write songs on a daily or weekly schedule and regularly produce and promote demo tapes of your work for artists, publishers, producers, and record companies. That's another reason why you should keep records of your correspondence as suggested in the first factor mentioned above.

Whether or not you earn a profit (or any money at all) from your songwriting activities is only one factor the IRS may consider in determining whether your efforts will be classified as a hobby or as a trade or business.

Remember, no single element described here will likely be conclusive in determining your tax status, and there are other factors I have not listed. It's best to try to establish as many elements of a trade or business as you can.

If you think your attorney or accountant may have been too conservative, limiting or eliminating your expense claims in the past because you were not making money from songwriting, and if you honestly believe you could establish that you're conducting yourself as a trade or business, instruct your advisor accordingly for your next tax return. If your attorney or accountant should disagree, without an explanation satisfactory to you, find a new financial advisor who specializes in entertainment matters (or is willing to do the necessary research to help you).

What Can You Deduct?

If your songwriting is a trade or business, what can you deduct, and how do you deduct it? Let's assume you've crossed the initial barrier, and you think you can firmly establish that your songwriting activities are a regular trade or business regardless of your income from your songs. What do you do?

Most importantly, as I mentioned earlier, get in the habit of keeping detailed records of *all* of your expenses. Common expenses of doing business as a songwriter might include tape costs, paper costs, telephone calls, the purchase or rental of musical instruments and recording equipment, education expenses, mileage (including driving to and from collaboration sessions, meetings of your local songwriter's association, or conferences with publishers, artists, managers, and record company personnel), and other travel and entertainment expenses. Depending on the status of the federal or state tax laws at a given time, you probably won't be able to deduct all of these things, but it's best to have available a complete record of expenses anyway.

Travel and entertainment expenses are a category that is most likely to face examination if the IRS ever audits your tax return, so be sure you make detailed notes of the business purpose of any trips, meals, or overnight hotel bills. When you travel to another city to promote your songs or attend a major industry event, keep accurate daily records of the names of people and companies you contacted or met with during your trip, and the nature of your discussions with them. It's then likely you'll be able to justify your claim of a business purpose for the expenses. Of course, there are many rules that may limit these kinds of expenses, such as specific limits on expenses for meals (when this chapter was written, the federal limit was 80 percent of the actual cost of the meal) and other, more general limits on meals and other entertainment claims (they must not be too expensive or otherwise extravagant under the circumstances).

Education expenses can present another problem. Suppose you take a songwriting course because you hope to write better songs that might be recorded by major artists. The federal law for many years has been that education expenses to "maintain or improve" your skills in your trade or business are deductible, while education expenses to qualify you for a new trade or business are *not* deductible. So again, whether or not your songwriting activities qualify you as being engaged in an existing trade or business makes the critical difference.

There are other important provisions of the tax laws allowing deductions for you only if you are in a trade or business. A significant example would be the interest you pay on a credit card purchase of a piece of musical equipment. In the major revision of the federal tax laws in 1986, the deduction for consumer interest was phased out, so that a decreasing percentage of these charges will be deductible on the tax returns of consumers purchasing, for example, clothes, cars, or television sets on credit. *The full deduction for interest on debt incurred in connection with a trade or business remains intact, though.* So again, as discussed earlier, if you believe you can prove you are a trade or business, be firm if your financial advisor tells you that the interest

Travel and entertainment expenses are a category that is most likely to face examination if the IRS ever audits your tax return, so be sure you make detailed notes of the business purpose of any trips, meals, or overnight hotel bills.

you're paying for your new guitar or synthesizer is only partially deductible. Otherwise, you'll lose a significant deduction when you buy equipment with a loan or other installment debt plan.

When Can Expenses Be Deducted?

Assuming your songwriting is a trade or business, can all expenses be deducted in the tax year during which they are incurred? With the exception of the cost of equipment purchased during a particular tax year (for example, musical instruments, recording studio equipment, computers, vehicles, etc.), virtually all other expenses have usually been deductible in the year they were incurred. Equipment has usually been "written off" over a longer period of time, using a combination of a tax credit in the first year of acquisition (as discussed earlier in this chapter, this is no longer available at present) and *depreciation* (this will be discussed later). Certain special provisions have allowed *accelerated* deductions or depreciation for equipment used in a trade or business. These laws permit you to deduct a larger portion of the cost in the early years of the *useful life* of the equipment.

This whole, comfortable scenario was drastically changed in 1986, however, when a potential economic disaster for songwriters was part of a major revision to the federal tax law (it has now been corrected by an amendment to that tax revision, but a similar law may again be passed in the future). For the first time, broad provisions of the law applying to the *capitalization* of expenses incurred in the manufacture of products for sale were applied to the creation of songs and demonstration recordings. Songwriters were considered the same as manufacturers of products for sale!

The disadvantage of this characterization was that costs incurred in the creation or recording of songs now had to be *capitalized*. This is a fairly complex concept, but in its simplest form, songwriters were now expected to predict the income-earning power of a song when it was created. They would then be allowed to deduct each year only that portion of expenses incurred previously for that song that matched the portion of income earned for the song in that year.

Under this unfortunate law, capitalization rules had to be applied to *all* expenses incurred in the creation and recording of songs. These included such items as tape costs, musical instruments, recording equipment, recording studio fees, and fees paid to musicians and singers for recording sessions. To make matters worse, a songwriter had to figure out how to allocate all of these expenses among all of the songs and demos created!

These recent, but now terminated, capitalization rules made songwriters, their attorneys, and their accountants furious, for a variety of reasons. First, the majority of songs created, even by the most successful songwriters, earn no money at all, so virtually all of the expenses incurred by songwriters for most songs would never be deductible. Second, who would ever be able to predict with any degree of accuracy the probable income for the life of a song's copyright? A songwriter creating a song is just not comparable to a company that manufactures a hammer, predicts the wholesale price the company will receive for the hammer, and deducts the expense of making the hammer when it is sold.

Thankfully, the capitalization rules have now been revised to exclude most creative professionals such as songwriters, authors, artists, and so on. In case this issue ever arises again, however, you'll at least have some understanding of the unfairness and can write to your congressman to complain!

Assuming normal deduction and depreciation rules for musical instruments and recording equipment are in effect as you read this, you should understand how to use them to your advantage. First, for many years there has been a special expense deduction for new equipment used in your trade or business and purchased during the tax year. This is now contained in Section 179 of the Internal Revenue Code. (I know I promised not to discuss specific laws, but if it's still in effect when you read this chapter, this section is too good to pass up!)

Under this provision, up to $10,000 worth of certain types of equipment acquired for use in your trade or business (cars and trucks are *not* included) may be *totally* written off in the first year, and no drawn-out process of depreciation will apply to such items. Be careful, though, because unlike deductions for your other songwriting expenses, *this deduction cannot exceed the total amount of taxable income derived from your songwriting during the tax year.* You can, however, "carry forward" to another year any portion of the expense that *would* have been deductible if you had earned enough taxable income from songwriting in the year you purchased the equipment.

Depreciation is simply an accounting method that allows you to deduct some percentage of the cost of a piece of equipment over what the Internal Revenue Code has determined is the *useful life* of that equipment. There are classification charts that list whether certain categories of equipment are considered to have a useful life of three, five, seven, ten, or more years.

There are a variety of depreciation methods available. The one that would be best for your tax situation should be determined with your accountant or other tax advisor, because there are various advantages and disadvantages of each. A simple explanation of some of the more commonly used methods might at least point you in the right direction and provide you with enough knowledge to ask the right questions.

> *Depreciation* is simply an accounting method that allows you to deduct some percentage of the cost of a piece of equipment over what the Internal Revenue Code has determined is the *useful life* of that equipment.

1. *The straight-line method.* Here, an equal percentage of the cost of the item (less salvage value) is deducted during each year of the useful life of the equipment. Under this method, the approximate salvage value of the equipment is subtracted from the purchase price (*not* deducted as an expense) *before* deductions are taken, because for most methods of depreciation, an asset cannot be deducted below its reasonable salvage value.

   For example, if you buy a $5,500 synthesizer that is considered to have a useful life of five years and an approximate salvage value of $500, you could deduct $1,000 each year. This method might best be used if you anticipate a relatively equal flow of income over the five-year period, and you want to make sure you have certain deductions in each of the five years to reduce your taxable income. (Remember, from the discussion earlier in the chapter, that reducing your taxable income may also reduce your tax bracket for that year.)

2. *The double-declining balance method.* Under this computation, 200 percent (double) of the straight-line method rate is used and applied to the remaining balance of the cost that has not been depreciated. For this method, the salvage value is not subtracted from the purchase price before depreciation, but the equipment may still not be depreciated below a reasonable salvage value. In the example of the $5,500 synthesizer, the allowable depreciation in the first

year would be $2,200 instead of $1,000 (if the straight-line rate had been applied to $5,500, the first year deduction would have been $1,100, so *double* that rate would be $2,200). In the second year, there would be $3,300 in value left to be depreciated ($5,500 minus $2,200). The normal five-year straight-line rate applied to $3,300 would be $660 per year, but under the double-declining balance method, $1,320 would be allowed (200 percent of $660). This computation might best be used when you anticipate a large amount of income over the first two or three years after a piece of equipment is purchased, but are uncertain as to your income level after that, because this method allows you to deduct a much larger percentage of the cost of a piece of equipment over those first few years. It is common tax strategy to maximize your deductions during your years of greatest income.

3. *The sum-of-the-years-digits method.* Under this computation, the depreciation you are allowed to take each year is computed by multiplying a changing fraction times the purchase price of the equipment less reasonable salvage value. The numerator of the fraction changes each year to represent the number of years remaining in the useful life of the equipment, and the denominator is always the sum of the numbers (digits) representing each of the years of the useful life. So in the synthesizer example ($5,500 piece of equipment, $500 salvage value, five-year useful life), the depreciation you would be allowed to take in the first year would be 5/15 of $5,000 (approximately $1,666), and in the second year you could deduct 4/15 of $5,000 (approximately $1,333). The "5" in the first year represented five years remaining of the synthesizer's useful life, and the "15" is simply 5+4+3+2+1, the *sum of the years digits*. This method seems to be best if you anticipate a slowly declining income level over the life of the piece of equipment, because it allows a slightly greater deduction in the first year but still allows deductions in the later years.

If you're totally confused by now, perhaps this chart will help:

Years	1st	2nd	3rd	4th	5th
Straight-Line Method Depreciation Deduction	$1,000	$1,000	$1,000	$1,000	$1,000
Double Declining-Balance Method Depreciation Deduction	$2,200	$1,320	$792	$475.20	$212.80*
Sum-of-the-Years Digits Method Depreciation Deduction	$1,666	$1,333	$1,000	$666	$333

*This would be the maximum depreciation allowed, because any further deduction would depreciate the synthesizer below its $500 reasonable salvage value.

My description of these basic (and not-so-basic) strategies by no means makes you an expert on depreciation. You should still see your accountant, because there are many other methods of depreciation under federal and state law that might be available to you. You will also need help in determining both the useful life and salvage value of the equipment you will be depreciating, because the IRS will not merely accept your estimate of these factors!

State Tax Laws

How do the tax laws of the states differ from federal tax laws? Many states adopt federal rules for deduction of most business expenses, but check with your financial advisor for the important exceptions where you live. California's rules for depreciation, for example, are totally different from the federal rules, although many other deductible items are allowed equally on both federal and California tax returns.

——

This chapter should have taught you some general ways to take advantage of the tax laws before they take advantage of you! Remember my caution at the beginning, though. These are only *general* tax principles. There are an unlimited number of exceptions and qualifications to all of the rules I've explained here, and federal and state tax laws are revised with alarming frequency. In this area of the law, there is no substitute for a professional, knowledgeable accountant or other tax advisor. If you find someone who knows the right rules and applies them properly, you have nothing to fear from the Internal Revenue Service.

CHAPTER 11

FOR A FEW DOLLARS MORE:
DEALING WITH INVESTORS

Y*ou* know you've got incredible talent and can write hit songs, even if the rest of the world hasn't found out yet. *You* know you will be a great success as a songwriter if you could just save enough money to have the time to do nothing but write for a few months. Or perhaps some better instruments or recording equipment for your demos would make the difference. Or enough studio time at the "right" studio. Or maybe all you need is the money to hire a great demo singer, a super producer, or some pro musicians to make your demos really sell your songs. How often have you said some of these things to yourself?

Unless you're independently wealthy, or unless you make enough money outside of songwriting to support your basic living expenses and songwriting activities, at some point you may have to rely upon money from relatives, friends, or even total strangers to pursue your dreams of songwriting success. Whether you use the extra money for food, rent, musical equipment, or the demos you need to convince the world of your talent, you're asking someone to make an investment in your future. Unfortunately, many of you might eagerly "sell your soul" for these critical dollars, giving away far too much in your intense desire to get ahead.

This chapter will discuss general strategies for compensating investors without jeopardizing your future through deals that sacrifice too much control or financial participation in your eventual success. The next chapter will be a close companion to this one, covering ways to compensate producers, singers, studio musicians, and recording studios with little or no cash up front. The object of both chapters is to help you finance your songwriting activities—either with someone else's money or no money at all.

Law and the Investor

Before discussing possible agreements with investors, you must first be aware that there are state and federal laws that might restrict how you can find ("solicit") your investors, the amount of money that can be raised, the number of investors who can be involved in a particular project, or even the kinds of people who can be investors. These laws require that investments not meeting certain criteria be registered with or *qualified* by some state or federal agency in order to be legal. That process can be a long and difficult one, and for the level of activity most of you will be pursuing, you will want to avoid any such requirements.

Before you start losing sleep over your current investment plans and running for

There are state and federal laws that might restrict how you can find your investors, the amount of money that can be raised, the number of investors who can be involved in a particular project, or even the kinds of people who can be investors.

the nearest attorney, you should feel safe in the knowledge that the majority of small investment deals you will become involved in are probably exempt (not covered by any law). So you can still go to Mom and Dad for the $2,000 you need for a four-song demo without going to jail. After hearing of some recent schemes by songwriters, however, I became aware that some of you might be too aggressive or successful with your investor strategies for your own good! One songwriter/artist I knew solicited investors in the *Wall Street Journal*! Another, through the work of friends and relatives, accumulated an assortment of fifteen to twenty strangers spread over six states.

The more public your quest for investors, the larger the amount of money that is invested, the greater the number of investors, the more strangers who are involved, and the more investors who live in other states, the more likely you may be violating some federal or state law. For example, you cannot merely place an ad in a national publication (or, in most states, even a local publication) stating "Investors Wanted for Recording Project." That might be considered a *public solicitation*, and any agreement with someone who responds to such an ad is probably illegal unless registered and qualified under both federal law and the law of the state in which the investor is a resident.

In general, your investment plan is most likely to be exempt from federal and state registration and qualification if the solicitation is totally private, the amount of money involved is low, the investors are few, and you either have a previous personal relationship or acquaintance with the investors or they (or their advisors) have some degree of business or financial sophistication. In many states, any one of these factors might be sufficient to exempt your investment proposal. The most common investment plans used by songwriters, those involving only relatives, friends, acquaintances, and moderate amounts of money ($1,000 to $25,000), are usually legal everywhere. If you have the slightest doubt, however, seek professional advice as to your plan. In most states, the amount of money being raised and the number of investors might be sufficient criteria to exempt your plan.

> In general, your investment plan is most likely to be exempt from federal and state registration and qualification if the solicitation is totally private.

Some specific examples might put your mind further at ease, but remember, as with other chapters of this book concerning tax laws and copyright laws, *any of these laws might change at any time*. Also, there are often further qualifications, exceptions, and detailed regulations affecting any laws. *Do not rely upon any specific laws discussed in this chapter without consulting an attorney*. The examples that follow are provided only to give you a general knowledge of the kinds of laws that exist and the broad areas they cover. (You've also just received a not-so-subtle lesson in the art of legal *disclaimers*!)

As this is written, the easiest federal exemptions for an investor plan are:

1. the entire *offering* (investment "shares" or investment agreements) is "sold" only to persons residing within one state, and that state is the same state where you are residing and doing business at the time you *sell* the investment (that is, offer and conclude the agreement and accept the cash); or

2. the offer and sale of the investment are made only outside of the United States to persons residing permanently (or for a long time) outside the United States so that the *security* you are selling *comes to rest* in a foreign country (that is, the investor will likely continue to reside in the foreign country while possessing the investment agreement).

Don't think your little one-page investment agreement won't fall within the complex, lengthy definition of a *security* under federal law. Contrary to what you might believe, securities do not only include stocks and bonds. Under most state and federal regulations, any agreement or other document providing someone with an ownership interest in a business (your songwriting) or with a continuing financial participation interest in that business could be a security. For example, a partnership interest is a security.

If you can't qualify for a total federal exemption under the provisions described above, there's still hope. If your investment plan involves less than $500,000 (I think it's safe to assume that most of you will be satisfied raising money below this amount), your plan may qualify for exemption under Regulation D of the Securities and Exchange Commission, but only if either:

A. you offer the investment in states that require registration of the security and delivery of *disclosure* documents to certain state authorities, and you comply with all such laws of the states involved; or

B. if the states involved do not require any registration and disclosure (which many will not require at low levels of investment), you do not offer or sell the investment by any form of general solicitation or general advertising, and you notify your investors that the investment is not registered under federal security laws and can't be resold to anyone else.

Disclosure under various state laws usually means providing the appropriate state authorities with all pertinent information about your proposed investment plan, and it will also often require the approval of that state authority. This is *not* an easy process, and you should make every attempt to be certain your intended investor strategy is exempt from state registration. In some states, if your intended sale of securities is significant enough to require registration and disclosure, you will have little chance of gaining approval. This is because most state regulatory agencies that review investment proposals will only approve the plans of well-established, well-financed businesses that have been in operation for many years.

If you haven't qualified for total exemption in (1) or (2) above, it should be obvious that alternative (B) will be the simplest for your purposes. Regardless of whether you use (A) or (B), however, there is still a technical, relatively simple federal requirement that you file certain notices with the Securities and Exchange Commission for the first sale of your investment security and the completion of all sales of your investment within a specific time period.

I'm *not* advising you to break the law, but despite the technical legal requirements I've outlined above, it's not likely the federal government or any state government will care about your investment plan if it's a small amount of money obtained from just a few people who are relatives, friends, or personal acquaintances, no matter how many states they live in. So it's still okay to ask Uncle Fred and Aunt Mildred for money, even if they live in Idaho. If you plan to go after a lot of strangers across state lines for large amounts of money, however, see an attorney!

The investment laws of California are an example of what a typical state law might be like, *but be sure to investigate the laws of your own state before you take any significant amount of money from anyone outside your immediate circle of relatives and friends*. Also, your state's investment laws might apply to your plan *regardless of whether you have complied with all federal regulations* (that's the way it is in California, for example). In California, your investment plan would be exempt from registration or qualification under state law only if *all* of the following circumstances are met:

1. Sales of the security must not be made to more than thirty-five persons, including those living outside the state. This is an easy requirement to meet, as I'm sure very few of you have the time or energy to try to convince thirty-five people that your songwriting talent is worth their money.

2. All purchasers must either have a pre-existing personal or business relationship with you, or, because of their business or financial expertise (or the expertise of their attorney or accountant), could reasonably be assumed to have the capacity to protect their own interests in the transaction. The best safeguard here (if you go beyond your immediate circle of friends and relatives), would be to make sure you have proof your investor consulted with an accountant or attorney experienced in business matters and investments in general, or the music business in particular. Save copies of correspondence from any attorney or accountant representing your investors so you can later prove they had sufficient advice and protection when they signed the agreement you proposed.

3. Purchasers must represent that they are purchasing your investment (the security) for their own account and cannot transfer it to anyone else. This is accomplished through a simple paragraph in your investment contract.

4. The offer and sale of the security may not be accomplished by publication of any advertisement. This is the easiest requirement of all. Just keep your proposal out of any publicly circulated newspaper, newsletter, or magazine, and don't post advertisements on bulletin boards or in other public places.

Legal Liabilities

Now you've learned that if you follow the laws concerning the offering of investments, you're on safe ground, right? Not quite. In addition to laws covering your general investment proposal, you must be careful not to create legal liability for yourself because of promises and other representations you've made to convince someone to give you money. It doesn't really matter whether the promises are written in the actual investment agreement, because you can sometimes be held responsible for oral statements.

For example, unless you intend that the money being given to you is only a loan, do not promise that specific amounts of money will be repaid at a certain time, or you could be legally liable for payment of that money. Additionally, although you don't want to discourage your investors, avoid unrealistic estimates of eventual profits. It's probably safest to avoid any written or oral income projection estimates at all.

Also, make sure your investors are aware there are no guarantees that your songs will earn any income whatsoever. It would be best to include this in your agreement as a specific disclaimer that warns something like, "Investor is hereby informed that music industry projects are extremely speculative, and that no amounts whatsoever are guaranteed to be repaid to the investor under this agreement." You should also make no type of representation or promise at all regarding the tax advantages or disadvantages of a particular investment. Merely tell your investors to consult with their own attorneys or accountants for the tax ramifications of the investment.

Investment Proposals

Now that you're aware of some basic legal pitfalls in dealing with investors, let's look at some general kinds of investment proposals. The specific terms you should offer to a particular investor will vary widely, depending upon who is providing the money and how much is being invested.

The basic structure of an investment deal can take many forms. The most complex involve the formation of corporations or partnerships to operate a music publishing company to own and control your copyrights and songwriting career. The simplest are merely loans for which you guarantee repayment of the money you've received within a definite time period (and usually with interest). The most common lie in between—a wide variety of participation formulas giving the investor the chance to financially participate in the income from some or all of your songs.

Whatever the form of the investment deal, no matter how much is being invested, no matter how badly you need the money, and no matter who is investing, these agreements should be carefully considered, drafted, and negotiated. Despite the fact that the vast majority of investment arrangements produce no financial results, you must presume the opposite—that you will become a major success in the music industry. You must therefore be careful to avoid agreements that can prevent your future artistic and financial success by giving away either too much control over your songs or too large a financial participation. From earlier chapters, it should be clear to you that you may need these rights for later, more important deals with recording artists, record companies, managers, producers, and publishers.

As a general rule, you should reject proposals that would transfer ownership or control over any of your copyrights or songwriting services to someone not professionally involved in the music industry on a full-time basis. For example, some investors (especially if they're represented by a music industry attorney) might insist upon single-song contracts or exclusive songwriter agreements (discussed in chapters six and seven) under which you would be employed by their "paper" publishing company (one that exists only for purposes of a contract). These types of agreements should virtually never be considered unless the investor is actually an active music publisher, personal manager, or record producer. You cannot afford to give away important rights and powers you should be granting to music industry professionals.

General partnerships and corporations (in which the investor might exercise joint control with you over your copyrights and songwriting services) are also not a good idea for the same reason. Your judgment as to the best use or deal for your songs might be very different from the opinion of someone not involved in the music industry, and you can't afford to have someone like that sharing the ownership and control of your songs. These types of situations are most often proposed by investors who are providing substantial sums of money (usually more than $25,000 to $50,000).

Another disadvantage of forming a partnership or corporation with an investor is that a variety of general business laws of your state will affect your rights, making the deal far more complex than you ever imagined and providing endless legal pitfalls. For example, if you sign an exclusive songwriter's agreement with a corporation

As a general rule, you should reject proposals that would transfer ownership or control over any of your copyrights or songwriting services to someone not professionally involved in the music industry on a full-time basis.

you formed with two investors, the songs you write will technically belong to the corporation and its shareholders, not to you as an individual (even though you're probably one of the shareholders). Depending on the agreement when you formed the corporation, if the corporation ever *dissolves* (terminates), its assets may have to be sold to outsiders. You may end up losing all rights to your own songs!

A major investor may prefer a corporation or partnership for a variety of reasons. For example, when a songwriter who is also a recording artist wants to independently release and promote records, an investor may have a legitimate desire to be part of an ongoing business. More commonly, an attorney or accountant may have advised the investor to set up such a business for tax purposes, because under the current state of federal law, an investor who is actively involved in a business that is losing money has more ways in which to deduct the losses from other earned income.

Other investors may want a *limited partnership*. In this form of business, under the laws of most states, the investor exercises virtually no control over the company and is exposed to only limited legal liability for the debts of the business.

Whatever the business entity requested by your investor, just remember to reject any requests for control over your songs and songwriting services by individuals not experienced in the music industry. Otherwise, you're likely to regret you ever asked for their money.

Structuring the Deal to Your Advantage

Normally, the type of investment deal most advantageous to you as a songwriter will be a simple investor's participation agreement. In these situations, you should negotiate what the investor will be paid based upon a formula and taking into account three factors.

The first is the percentage. Will the investor receive 5 percent, 10 percent, 15 percent, 25 percent, or more? This is an extremely elementary concept. Keep the percentage as low as possible! The result of your negotiation for the next two factors will also affect the percentage.

The second factor is to determine what the percentage will apply to. If an investor gives you $500 to produce one song demo, should the investor receive a percentage of all the songs you write during the next five years? I don't think so. Try to limit investment participation to the specific project for which you used the investor's money. Naturally, at higher levels of investment, the investor may make the argument that a larger participation is justified. For example, if an investor gives you enough money for twenty song demos, and you sign an exclusive songwriter agreement with a major publisher based on those demos, it could be reasonably argued that the investment helped establish your songwriting career.

The third factor is the *ceiling* or limit on the investor's participation. This could be a dollar amount (for example, double or triple the initial investment), or it could designate a period of time after which the investor is no longer paid. The lower the investment, the more justified you are in insisting upon a lower ceiling. The investment of $500 for a single song demo might be worth a participation interest that ends after the investor has been paid $1,000 or $1,500. I realize that sounds very high, bearing in mind that it appears to be an interest rate of 100 percent or 150 percent, but remember that an investment in your songs is not as secure as a bank certificate of deposit or corporate bond. The vast majority of songs never earn ten cents, so you

An investment in your songs is not as secure as a bank certificate of deposit or corporate bond, so you will probably need to offer a high potential return to attract an investor's interest.

will probably need to offer a high potential return to attract an investor's interest. If this were a straight loan, you would guarantee payment, the risk would be minimal for the investor, and you would only offer an interest rate slightly above what a bank would charge for a loan.

So, as an example applying all three factors at once, if an investor is willing to give you $2,000 for a four-song demo, you can offer to pay 25 percent of the income you earn from those four songs until the investor has been paid $4,000. You are offering a 100 percent return on the investment (double the investor's money), because you understand that the investment is highly risky. A *sliding scale* is also commonly used for investments. In the example above, you can offer to pay the investor 50 percent of the income from the four songs until they are repaid their initial $2,000, 25 percent until you've paid another $1,000, and 15 percent until you've paid the final $1,000.

Under the three-factor formula I've proposed, if the investor has demanded one factor that is unreasonably high, try to adjust some other factor to compensate. If the investor insists upon no ceiling, for example, (a position you should only accept if large amounts of money are being invested), offer a lower percentage (5 percent or less). If the investor demands a higher percentage, lower the monetary ceiling or propose a time limit (which is just a different kind of ceiling). If the investor wants an unreasonably high percentage and no ceiling, make the percentage apply to videocassette sales in Nicaragua! The point is to make sure your investors are compensated for their risk without taking away too much of either your income or the income rights you may later need to give to a music publisher.

When discussing the area of an investor's income, it is best to give a percentage of the income *you* receive. If you don't define this carefully, and if you have granted to the investor a percentage of the overall or *gross* music publishing income, *your* income share will be reduced even more than normal when you make any kind of music publishing assignment to someone else. In fact, if you get too generous and are not very careful with an investment agreement, you might be receiving a lower share of the money from your song than is anyone else!

For example, suppose you have given an investor 50 percent of the overall gross music publishing receipts from a particular song. Then you sign a standard, single-song music publishing agreement with a music publisher (discussed in chapter six), under which you have assigned the right to 50 percent of the song's income. You will now receive fifty cents for every dollar received by the music publisher, but you will still owe the investor fifty cents because you failed to limit the investor's participation to your *net* receipts (after deductions by outside parties). You get to keep nothing!

You should now understand the basic potential traps of investment deals, as well as some negotiating strategies to avoid trouble. Now all you need is to find someone interested in giving you enough money to do what you want! Good luck!

CHAPTER 12

SPEC DEMOS:
HOW TO ATTRACT TALENT WITHOUT CASH

Now that you know what kinds of deals to offer an investor, what if you can't find anyone interested in risking money on your songs? How can you manage to get demos made without cash? This chapter will cover the kinds of deals to offer producers, singers, musicians, arrangers, and recording studios when you don't have enough money to hire them and can't get it from anyone else.

These are *spec* (speculative) deals. In a spec situation, you will be using the performances, services, facilities, or equipment of people who believe in the probable future success of your recording project (other than you!) and will accept payment when the songs eventually earn income. They are speculating that they will someday receive income or some other benefit that will make it worth the time and effort they spent.

For business purposes, there are really two different categories of spec demonstration recordings. The first category includes simply the song demos you make to promote yourself as a songwriter to record producers, recording artists, publishers, record companies, or personal managers. (I will refer to these recordings as *song demos* throughout this chapter.) With the increasing availability of affordable, professional-quality audio equipment, song demos are often produced in home studios. For the purposes of this chapter, however, I will assume you will need the services of someone other than yourself to complete your song demo project.

The second category of spec recordings is *master demos*. These are intended for either the independent release and sale of records featuring you as a songwriter/artist or for submission to record companies for a potential exclusive artist's agreement. In reality, many songwriters produce song demos that are better than some other songwriter/artist's master demos. Also, many songwriter/artists use the same demo as both a song demo and a master demo. For the purpose of this discussion, though, I think it will be clearer if the potential negotiations and agreements for each type of demo are covered separately.

Song Demos

The easiest and cheapest way to compensate someone for working on your demo is by trading services. Assuming you have a talent others may need someday for *their* demos, offer to exchange your services for theirs. So if you're a songwriter who's also a keyboard player, and if you know another songwriter who's a good guitar player,

> The easiest and cheapest way to compensate someone for working on your demo is by trading services. Assuming you have a talent others may need someday for *their* demos, offer to exchange your services for theirs.

you could both perform on each other's demos at no charge. Or perhaps you know singers who would perform on your demos if you agree to either perform on their recording artist demos or collaborate with them to create better songs for their repertoire.

The next best way to compensate a producer, singer, musician, arranger, engineer, or recording studio without cash is very similar to the participation agreement covered in the last chapter for cash investors. The main difference is that you will consider the performance, service, recording facility, or equipment as the investment (instead of actual cash). You will then calculate some cash value for this kind of investment, and you'll pay this investor based upon that cash value just as you would have paid a cash investor in the last chapter. (If you need to, refer to that chapter for a discussion of the basic investor's formula that includes a percentage, the basis for the percentage, and limits on the amount of money that will be paid.)

For example, if a producer's normal rate for a song demo is $500, you can consider that as a $500 cash investment. Then, just as you might with a cash investor, you can offer to pay the producer 10 percent of the income you receive from the song until you've paid $1,500. As with cash investors, sliding scales can also be used in this situation. The spec participation in the previous example could be designed to pay 25 percent until the producer has received $500, 15 percent until an additional $500 has been paid, and 5 percent until the balance has been received by the producer. If a producer insists on higher dollar limits, offer a lower percentage.

You must always try to save sufficient income rights to your songs, and *all* rights of ownership and control, for more important deals later in your career.

You can use the same formula for anyone else providing performances, services, or equipment for a song demo. If a session guitar player would normally charge you $50 per hour, the total hours will give you the total investment. If a recording studio would have charged $100 per hour for the studio and $20 per hour for the engineer, computing the total of what the charges would have been for your use of their facilities and personnel would be equal to the value of their investment.

Another possible alternative for a limit or ceiling on the payback for spec services or facilities would be to limit the payments to a specific time period. For instance, you could agree that the entire payment formula only applies if there is a commercial recording of the song within one year after the completion of the song demo, arguing that if there are no results by such time, you will be recording a new song demo. You could also limit the payment formula to sums received by you from exploitation of the song within two or three years after completion of the song demo or after the song is first commercially recorded and released for sale.

As with cash investors, be careful to calculate how much you will be giving away *before* you start to make your spec deals. Obviously, you can't give four different people 50 percent of the song! In my opinion, you should always limit the total, combined financial participation for *all* investors to no more than 50 percent, regardless of whether you are dealing with cash investors or the types of noncash investors discussed in this chapter. Your object is to personally receive at least as much money as all of the investors together.

Depending upon the cash or cash value invested, some investors will insist that they be paid 100 percent of your receipts until they have received the value of what they have given you (this is called being paid "off the top" until the investment is recouped by the investor). If you accept this proposal, be sure that the participation percentage paid to your investors is substantially lower after the point of recoupment. Otherwise, it may be too many years before you enjoy any substantial profits from your work.

Dealing with Music Industry Professionals

There is a major difference between dealing with cash investments and people who will provide the kind of services and facilities I'm discussing in this chapter. You are now doing business with music industry professionals, and many of them (especially producers) may want a much larger participation in your future success in exchange for the risk they are taking that they will never be repaid. For example, producers or recording studios that have devoted many hours to long-term, twenty-song demo projects might insist that there be no ceiling as to either the potential money they can receive or the time period during which they will receive it. Other producers or recording studios might ask for all or part of the ownership and control of the publishing rights to the songs recorded.

Even though you are now negotiating with people active in the music industry (or, I should say, *especially* when you are working with people active in the music industry), you must still be very cautious before agreeing to these types of arrangements. One of the same basic negotiating rules discussed in the last chapter still applies: You must always try to save sufficient income rights to your songs, and *all* rights of ownership and control, for more important deals later in your career.

An assignment of some or all of the publishing rights to a producer might be appropriate if: (a) the producer is an established music publisher who will aggressively promote the song or songs involved; or (b) the producer is a record producer for major acts and has promised to use one or more of the songs in an upcoming project. In that kind of situation, *this* might be the important deal in the development of your career! Regardless, as I mentioned in the discussion of single-song agreements in chapter six, always get a reversion clause reassigning all rights for a particular song to you if that song is not used in some specific manner within a definite time period that is designated in the agreement.

With the exception of the situations above, unless you are a songwriter/artist who intends that the production project will be used for direct submission to record companies for an exclusive artist's agreement, try to be firm in rejecting a spec producer who insists upon publishing rights or refuses any limits as to financial participation in your eventual success. As to recording studios, singers, musicians, arrangers, and engineers involved in your demo, in my opinion, it's virtually never appropriate

It's very difficult to convince talented people or desirable recording studios to give free services or facilities to speculate on your success. You may have to be extremely flexible and creative in your deal-making to obtain their involvement.

to assign any portion of music publishing ownership or control to any of them. Such demands may cost you far more than the services, performances, or facilities were worth, and you will probably be able to find other people to provide services and facilities of equal value to your song demos on better financial terms.

Now that I've taught you how to be tough in your negotiations, remember that it's often very difficult to convince talented people or desirable recording studios to give free services or facilities to speculate on your success. You may have to be extremely flexible and creative in your deal-making to obtain their involvement.

Master Demos

When you decide to record master demos that will be sold to the public or *shopped* (promoted) to record companies for a potential exclusive artist's agreement, you will usually face a more complex negotiation when trying to get someone to give you spec performances, services, or facilities. This is because anyone with even the most basic knowledge of the music industry knows the potential financial rewards are much greater if you become successful as a recording artist rather than a nonperforming songwriter. This prospect can work to your advantage, though, because if people believe strongly enough in your talent as a songwriter/artist, they will be willing to devote greater amounts of time and effort and take greater risks for your recording projects.

There are two general purposes for master demos, and each requires different strategies and formulas for compensating those who have become speculatively involved in production. You or your producer might promote the master demos directly to record companies for a recording artist agreement, or you may decide to independently release recorded products for sale to the public.

Promotion to Record Companies

Even though some labels refuse to accept unsolicited material that has not been submitted by a personal manager, producer, or attorney they know, most major record companies still receive tremendous numbers of master demos for their consideration. It is therefore crucial that your tape make an impact that distinguishes it from the others. In addition to great songs, this uniqueness is most frequently the result of the production sound of the music and vocals—a sound that creates a distinct artistic identity.

The Producer's Role
The producer's role in capturing or creating an artistic identity on tape is by far the most critical of all the assistance you will need for distinctive master demos. The producer's importance in the music industry is similar to that of the director's in the motion picture industry—the best can enhance and maximize talent with artistic vision and production skills, while the worst can destroy it. For this reason, we should first discuss the producer's compensation.

Your producer could be your songwriting collaborator, a member of your band, a recording studio engineer, an actual professional producer with credits, or some other person with production experience. Whoever it is, before you record anything, you should discuss mutual plans and perceptions about the project and finalize your business arrangements.

The best producers will have all the work they can handle at their normal hourly rates, so it's unlikely they would become involved in your project on a speculative basis unless they thought you were going to be a major star. If they do become involved with you, though, *and if they will also be actively promoting the project to record labels*, they may insist that you sign a *production agreement* with their production company, as well as requiring an assignment of all or some portion of your music publishing rights.

Production Agreements

Production agreements are the highest level of spec agreements for producers (and also potentially the most financially rewarding for them). They are essentially exclusive recording artist contracts where you are employed by the producer or the producer's production company. The producer, not you, will usually have the power to make decisions concerning your recorded performances and will then present the whole package (that is, producer and songwriter/artist) to a record label.

That kind of deal probably sounds like nothing you'd ever want, because you've learned throughout this book about reserving all of your rights to ownership and control for more important deals later. What if a particular producer has the clout and connections to make this your important deal? Regardless, some attorneys would advise you *never* to sign this kind of agreement. I don't agree with that advice, because production agreements like these do sometimes result in success. You should, however, be *extremely* selective in accepting such an arrangement.

Suppose you agree to a production deal because this producer has produced two platinum albums over the past three years. How does this type of situation work?

If you are a songwriter/artist who is signed to a record label through a production company, you will not be paid directly by the record company. Instead, the record label will pay all advances, royalties, recording budgets, and other sums directly to the producer, who will then pay you some percentage of these receipts. Typically, the split of sums paid by the record company to the producer is 50 percent to the producer and 50 percent to the artist, although some producers will agree to retain only 40 percent, and some will insist they keep as much as 60 percent. This split should apply to all monies paid by the record company that are not spent for some purpose designated by the record company (for example, the recording budget provided for an album).

Just like the reversion clause in a single-song agreement, this kind of agreement should have a set time limit for specific results. For example, if the producer has not been able to obtain an exclusive recording artist's agreement for you with a major label within one year, the agreement should end, and you should be free to record for someone else.

If the producer also insists that you assign some or all of your music publishing rights, try to resist this proposal by adopting a tough negotiating posture. If that doesn't work, try to limit the deal to cover only co-publishing or administration rights (discussed in chapter six). You should also insist that any music publishing assignment be limited to songs recorded and released for sale under an agreement between the production company and a major record company.

The financial value producers will place on their services is likely to be substantially higher for master demos than song demos.

If you have retained a producer who will *not* be actively promoting your master demos for a record deal, let's go back to our original stance—you should never sign a production agreement or give away any ownership or control of your music publishing rights. Instead, first suggest the identical payment formula discussed earlier in this chapter for song demos. Be aware, however, that the financial value producers will place on their services is likely to be substantially higher for master demos than song demos. This is because a greater degree of creativity is probably involved, as well as a substantially greater amount of time and effort.

Payment Formulas

As an alternative to the spec payment formula discussed in the last chapter and earlier in this chapter, an agreement with a spec producer of master demos should always provide for the possibility that the actual master demos will be used as masters by a record company for the manufacture of recorded products. Therefore, you need to put in writing the percentage you will pay the producer from royalties you might eventually receive from a record company.

The most common form of royalty paid to artists signed directly to a record label is an *all-in royalty*, which is intended to cover the services of both the artist and producer. In a *direct signing* situation (as opposed to artists signing to record companies through the producer's production company, described above), the artist has the power to determine how much of this royalty will be paid to the producer. In this situation, you should pay the producer participation *points* of the all-in royalty. (*Points* are merely percentage points but are described this way to avoid confusion. For example, if a record company is paying you an all-in royalty of 10 percent of the suggested retail price for albums sold, and you want to pay your producer a royalty of 3 percent, this is described as three points of your royalty, not 3 percent of your royalty.)

For record labels that base their royalty structure on some version of the retail price of recorded products sold, most producers are generally paid in the range of three to five points of an all-in royalty. For record labels that base their royalty structure on some version of the wholesale price of recorded products sold, most producers are paid six to ten points of the all-in royalty. Your agreement with your producer should provide for either situation, because you won't know what your royalty basis will be until you've seen the record company's agreement, and you won't see the record company agreement until you know which record company will be interested in signing you!

For producer royalties based upon what a record company will be paying you, keep the description of the royalty calculation as simple as I've described above. Also specify that the royalty you pay the producer will be computed in the same manner and at the same time as that paid to you by the record company. Otherwise, you might owe the producer money you haven't received! For example, don't promise a producer that you will pay 3 percent of the suggested retail price on 100 percent of all albums sold, because the record company that signs you may only pay you based on 85 percent of all albums sold and may substantially reduce your royalty rates on a variety of different sales categories.

The royalty computation you should give your producer will differ in one important respect from the one a record company will give to you. Recording costs are usually recouped by the record company only from your share of royalties, not the producer's. This means that even though you should not have to pay the producer royalties until the record company begins paying you royalties (because until your advances have been recouped by the record company, you will have no money to pay any royalties), when you *do* start receiving royalties, it is fairest to pay the producer on sales retroactively back to the first record sold. For example, if your royalty rate is one dollar per record, and if the record company has spent $100,000 in recording costs for your album, you will not received any royalties until the sale of record 100,001. If your producer's royalty rate is twenty-five cents per record (payable by you from your all-in rate), you will owe your producer the first $25,000 you receive in royalties to compensate for the first 100,000 copies sold.

In the case of spec producers, even if the actual masters they've produced for you are not released for sale or otherwise commercially exploited, it might still be fair to allow them to participate financially in any record company agreement you obtain with those master recordings. You could either refer to the spec formula in the section on song demos for some ideas or pay the producer some reduced share of the normal producer's rate for master recordings. For example, you could offer 50 percent of a normal rate by paying 1½ percentage points of any royalty based on a retail price and 3 percentage points of any royalty based on a wholesale price.

Other limits you might impose on a spec producer's participation could be to restrict payment solely to the exploitation of the songs and master demos produced by that producer. You could also place a time limit on financial participation, as with song demos, arguing that if no exclusive artist's agreement has been offered to you within one year to eighteen months, new master recordings will have to be produced. Another alternative would be to grant the spec producer a financial participation in only the first album released under the recording contract or to restrict the producer's financial participation to royalties received by you in the first two or three years of your exclusive artist's agreement with the record label.

Don't Guarantee Future Involvement

Unless you've agreed to a production agreement (where you are really working for the producer), *do not, under any circumstances, guarantee that the producer of the master demos will be retained by you or your eventual record company to produce your first single, first EP (extended play record), first album, or any other record company product*. Most record companies invest large sums of money to record and promote new acts, so they demand approval of any producer and may reject your choice. A common compromise here is a *buyout*. You could promise to use "best efforts" to have the producer approved by the record company to produce you, but if the record company refuses, you pay a specified sum to the producer (which should be recoupable from any other financial participation the producer will receive from sales of records). In this event, be careful not to promise too large a sum, because the advance you receive from the record company may not be enough to cover this guaranteed payment.

What about musicians, background singers, arrangers, and recording studios that may have worked on spec for your master demos? First of all, whether these are your best friends or casual acquaintances, you should politely explain the harsh reality of dealing with a record company, and you must decline their requests that you guarantee a particular role for them in your eventual recording project with the record label. Your eventual record producer simply may not want to use the guitarist, drummer, or recording studio that was involved with your initial master demos.

The best repayment plan would be the one I described in the section above on song demos. Additionally, if an actual master demo is used to make recorded products for release and sale to the public, you could promise to repay any session vocalists or musicians the applicable *union scale* for their services that would have been due under the rules of the American Federation of Musicians (AFM) or the American Federation of Television and Radio Artists (AFTRA).

Independent Sale of Records

Increasing numbers of artists attempt to sell records on their own in hopes of generating sufficient sales to attract the interest of a major label. Some major acts, such as Missing Persons, Heart, Motley Crue, and Quarterflash, were initially discovered and signed partly as a result of this strategy.

To pay a producer for this type of exploitation, it's probably best to compute a royalty based upon the suggested retail price of the products sold. There are two reasons for this. First, the distribution network for this kind of product is not often well organized unless an experienced independent distributor is used, so it may be difficult to compute any consistent wholesale selling price upon which to base a producer's royalty. Second, the reality is that many records may be sold directly by an artist to the public at live performances.

As with the royalties you would pay if the master demos were released by a record company, the range for producers should be 3 to 5 percent of the suggested retail list price, although some superstar producers may command a higher royalty. As a possible alternative, to avoid the complications of computing accurate retail prices for the independent sale of your records, you could offer the producer a percentage of your gross receipts from record sales. Using this method, a fair compensation percentage would be 15 to 25 percent of your gross receipts, although you should expect some producers to require a larger percentage.

As for musicians, singers, arrangers, and recording studios, I again suggest that the best payment methods are contained in the section on song demos. The limits on participation (the ceilings) are particularly important, because the contributions of these individuals and businesses are usually not significant enough to justify a perpetual royalty on the sale of products that use your songs or master recordings.

Finding talented people, especially producers, to become involved with your demo projects without initial cash payments can be a difficult and frustrating process. If you can convince others of your talent, though, and if you use the tips contained in this chapter, you may find it much easier to attract the kind of individuals and studios you need to advance your career.

JUST ONE LAST CHORUS

Look at what you've learned! You should now be able to avoid rip-offs aimed at songwriters, negotiate the major terms of your agreements, handle your own music publishing, and recognize significant areas of the copyright law that can protect your songs (or punish you for using too much from another song). The next time you deal with a music publisher, another songwriter, or someone who wants to use your music for some purpose, you should be completely confident that you know what you're doing.

Remember, though—you're still not an attorney, so don't write your own agreements. Just because you've learned to recognize when you have appendicitis, you're not ready to buy a scalpel and remove your own appendix!

Now, put this book down and get back to writing great songs!

Index

OTHER BOOKS TO HELP YOU MAKE MONEY AND THE MOST OF YOUR MUSIC TALENT

The Craft & Business of Songwriting
John Braheny
A powerful, information-packed (and the most up-to-date) book about the songwriting industry which thoroughly covers all the creative and business aspects that you need to know to maximize your chances of success. 322 pages/$19.95

The Craft of Lyric Writing
Sheila Davis
Davis, a successful lyricist, composer, and teacher, presents the theory, principles, and techniques that result in lyrics with timeless appeal. 350 pages/$18.95

Successful Lyric Writing:
A Step-by-Step Course & Workbook
Sheila Davis
A practical, self-contained lyric writing course, complete with exercises and lyric writing assignments designed to stimulate your creativity and build writing skills. 304 pages/$16.95, paperback

Getting Noticed:
A Musician's Guide to Publicity & Self-Promotion
James Gibson
Gibson helps performing musicians create effective yet inexpensive publicity materials, then use them to *get noticed* and *make money* with their music. 224 pages/$12.95, paperback

Making Money Making Music
(No Matter Where You Live)
James Dearing
Dearing shows you how to build a successful music career in any community—playing clubs, performing radio and TV jingles, operating a record studio, teaching, and selling lyrics through the mail. 305 pages/$12.95, paperback

The Performing Artist's Handbook
Janice Papolos
Practical know-how classical musicians need to progress in their professional music careers. 219 pages/$12.95, paperback

The Songwriter's Guide to Making Great Demos
Harvey Rachlin
From how to judge if a song is ready to be pitched to exactly how to produce a multitrack recording, covers every step of the process of making great demos. 192 pages/$12.95, paperback

Writing Music for Hit Songs
Jai Josefs
Professional songwriter Jai Josephs shows how to musically craft successful popular songs. His easy-to-understand explanations are illustrated with more than 170 musical examples from today's top artists. 256 pages/$17.95

Making It in the New Music Business
James Riordan

The coauthor of *The Platinum Rainbow* shows how to achieve success as a recording artist by building your own path to success. 377 pages/$18.95

The Songwriter's Guide to Collaboration
Walter Carter

A complete guide to all aspects of co-writing songs, from working relationships to legal and financial arrangements. 178 pages/$12.95, paperback

How to Pitch & Promote Your Songs
Fred Koller

For songwriters who want to make a full-time living with their music, a step-by-step guide to self-employment. 144 pages/$12.95, paperback

You Can Write Great Lyrics
Pamela Phillips Oland

Inside advice from one of today's top songwriters on how you can write lyrics with commercial appeal and focus on writing songs that have what it takes to succeed. 192 pages/$17.95, paperback

Protecting Your Songs & Yourself
Kent J. Klavens

A practical, thorough, easy-to-read guide to copyright, contracts, taxes, and other songwriting legal topics. 112 pages/$15.95, paperback

Gigging:
The Musician's Underground Touring Directory
Michael Dorf & Robert Appel

2,000 contacts to help you/your group book a regional or cross country tour and/or get airplay for your records. 224 pages/$14.95, paperback

1990 Songwriter's Market
edited by Mark Garvey

This annual directory is designed to help you make the right contacts! Includes 2,000 listings of music publishers, record companies/producers, advertising agencies, audiovisual firms, managers, booking agents, and play producers. You'll also find helpful articles on the business of songwriting, interviews with professionals in the industry, and lists of clubs, contests, and associations. 528 pages/$18.95

A complete catalog of all Writer's Digest Books is available FREE by writing to the address shown below. To order books directly from the publisher include $3.00 postage and handling for one book, 50¢ for each additional book. Allow 30 days for delivery.

Writer's Digest Books
1507 Dana Avenue
Cincinnati, Ohio 45207

Credit card orders call TOLL-FREE
1-800-289-0963

Prices subject to change without notice